The Absent Kids

Laura May Fleming

TABLE OF CONTENTS

ACKNOWLEDGEMENTS

I'd like to give a shout-out to a few special people who made this book possible, in alphabetical order:

Kerri Bell, Anne Brown, Kevin Carney, Dino Doularis, Doreen Doularis, Dakota Fleming, Marc "with a C" Fleming, Linda Gliatta, Michael Gliatta, Karen Kincaid, Marima (Meemaw), Jason Pesch, Jeimmy Quintero, Toni Rose, Larry Sharkey, Matthew Shock, Michele Shock, Bobby Steele, Diana Steele, David Wamsley, and Willie Wilson.

INTRODUCTION

As a small child, I was taught to always "live within my means", meaning my parents were too cheap to buy me the things I wanted, because they preferred to spend their money on drugs. After all, why buy a new doll house for their third child (who they said was a mistake), when they could get high instead? The routine was simple: the drug dealer would call and they would rush out the door. Sometimes, they would take me with them, to get what they called "medicine". Even at only five years old, I knew they were lying, and I knew it was something bad. I could feel it. I didn't need a teacher or a parent to teach me right from wrong. I simply knew. My parents taught me very little, so it amazes me how much I know. It's as if I was reincarnated and somehow brought my "smarts" with me from a past life. Or, maybe not; who knows? But, having always been reminded back in my childhood days, that I was a mistake, really bothered me. I've never spoken much about it until now. Here's the deal: my mother wanted a girl and she was blessed with my sister, her first child. Then, she decided she wanted a boy. Her wish was granted when my brother was born. She was done and got her tubes tied. But, seven years later... Oops. Either the operation had gone wrong, or *my* God had decided she wasn't done. Because if she had gotten her way, as she often did, you wouldn't be reading this.

But, I'm getting ahead of myself. This is the first book I've ever written. I have no clue if I will even finish it, or if it will be published, or what it's going to be about once it's done. But, that's what I love about writing it. You, my readers, will go on this journey with me. To me, that's exciting because I know my imagination is wild. It will be a mixture of fiction and non-fiction, horror and suspense; most likely all the above, because my life experiences are like no other. I simply can't make some of this stuff up. I exaggerate at times, for effect. But, there is some truth in everything I write. I hope this becomes one of those books you can't put down, or at least a book you really look forward to picking back up, to see what happens next. Time will tell. I just hope it doesn't become one of those books collecting dust, being sold at a garage sale for twenty-five cents, or even worse, in a box of stuff being given away for free. I promise you this, though: You will read about all the things I've never wanted anyone to know about, a lot of personal stuff. And,

I hope to be talked about. Even if people say negative stuff, that's fine by me. To me, I'll be like, "Yay! At least I'm being acknowledged as a person, instead of 'a mistake'." As I've gotten older, I've stopped caring about anything negative said about me anyway.

1 THE RAPE

The phone rang. *Here we go again!* I thought. My parents looked at each other with those half-ass smiles and their eyes told each other, *Yup, we'll be getting high today.* For me, it meant I would be sent to my bedroom, even if I hadn't done anything bad, and even if it was 9:30 a.m. Those fucking junkies. Why did I have to be punished for their sins? Why did my parents choose to invest in something that would disappear after only an hour or so? Instead, why not buy me a doll house that would last years? The times they would make me go with them, to pick up their drugs, were awful. I wished they would simply forget me and leave me home alone. It was an hour-long drive in a van with no back windows, so it always made me feel nauseous. When we would finally arrive in Paterson, New Jersey, I would have to hold my nose to avoid the nasty smell inside the project elevators. I would try to make eye contact with one of my parents, so they would see my reaction. I suppose it didn't smell too bad. But, holding my nose was my silent way of showing my parents I felt uncomfortable. It didn't work. They didn't notice, or even looked at me. They were too anxious for the elevator to arrive at the twenty-second floor, to apartment 227.

They would get so angry when the elevator made stops to pick up other passengers. They didn't want to wait a minute longer than they had to, to get high. It was their time, not some stranger's. If they had gotten their way, everyone else would have had to take the stairs. When we got off the elevator, my mother would put a blindfold on me. It didn't occur to me until later in life, why I wasn't allowed to see. It turns out, it was one of the drug dealer's rules, if a child was brought along. He didn't want to be identified or busted

3

by a young brat, if questioned by a police officer. An adult knew better, but a child didn't know how to be careful when answering questions from authorities. In the 1970s, or at least in my family, children were to be seen but not heard. Each time I wore the blindfold, my mother told me we were playing a game called, "See no evil, hear no evil, speak no evil." She told me, to be allowed to play, I must wear a blindfold. I guess it was okay to see, hear and speak evil behind closed doors, but not outside of the house. To me, where we lived wasn't a home. It was just a house: a place I would stay until it was legal for me to leave at age eighteen. Or, so I had been told.

I wanted to run away so badly. I wanted to live like my kindergarten classmates lived. They received hugs, kisses, and lots of toys and pets. I wasn't even allowed to have a goldfish. I knew better than to complain or compare, though. The one time I did, I got hit with a *Great Adventure* cutting board. It was the worst spanking ever, and my ass was red for weeks. It had looked like a first-degree sunburn, and I had never wanted to go to that amusement park ever again. It was the 'worst adventure' in my eyes, because of their logo on that cutting board. Like, when you have a hangover and see a T-shirt with *Miller Lite* printed on it. I didn't want any memory of something that had made me feel so awful inside. My timing was definitely off whenever I whined, or threw a tantrum, or whenever I complained about something dumb when my parents were coming down from one of their highs. I never wanted to give them a reason to take anything out on me, again. Sometimes they didn't need a reason though. I was simply in the wrong place at the wrong time: my own house.

The elevator door would open on the twenty-second floor and we would make a quick left. My mother would have her hands on my shoulders, directing me as I walked because I was always blindfolded. One time, there was an argument going on behind the door to apartment 227. It was loud, but it certainly didn't stop my dad from knocking. Even though I don't call my mother, 'Mom', I do call my father, 'Dad'. That's because Dad was much nicer to me than my mother. But, I've hardly ever been able to bring myself to call him 'Daddy' either. He was definitely the lesser of two evils, but he was still unfit.

There were a lot of things being thrown in apartment 227. I heard glass breaking, plus many bad words. I wished I couldn't hear instead of not being able to see, because what I was hearing was scary. The blindfold hid my tears. If it hadn't been on, I wouldn't have cried. The rule always applied: I was to be seen but not heard. A few minutes later, the yelling suddenly stopped. The door made a creaking noise as it slowly opened, and a man's voice said, "You shouldn't have knocked fifty-plus times. Sold out!" Before my mother could get all worked up though, the man continued, "Just kidding, what's the password?"

"The password is Luna, short for lunatic," my dad said. I was confused, not knowing how someone could make a not-so-funny joke after all of that yelling. I suppose that drug dealer had a dark sense of humor. Without telling me what was happening first, my dad slid his hands under my arms and lifted me up and put me on his shoulders. I kicked him in the stomach on the way, a normal reflex, but told him I was sorry. "It's okay, baby girl," he said. "I just want you to sit on my shoulders." My blindfold loosened a bit during the transfer, and I could see a tiny bit when I looked down. All I saw was broken glass on the floor. That's when I knew the reason he had put me on his shoulders. They hadn't had time to put my shoes on me after receiving the phone call, so I was barefoot. Putting my sneakers on would have taken away too much of their "get high" time. I was confused about why the yelling had stopped so suddenly. But, then it occurred to me: this was a business; an illegal drug business, but still a business. We were customers and they knew their customers would always come back, no matter what. There was no need to do returns in this business, because the customer always ended up happy and always came back for more. Only some customers got credit; not by their credit score, just by word of mouth. They kept it somewhat professional, and very discreet. Everyone knew, "snitches get stitches". In some cases, even death. You didn't want to stab these people in the backs, or ever take a plea if caught. Their game was to do evil. But, if you spoke or heard about where the evil came from, you had better run away *fast*. Jail was the worst place you could end up. They'd know the second you got out. You were safer in prison if you had a big mouth.

Much to my surprise, I heard through a microphone: "Test. One, two, one, two." Then, someone sang:

Welcome to the place where you come to buy things that will make you forget,

The place where you go when you're not entertained by your television set.

Allow us to make reality disappear.

Come back when it's all gone.

We never sell out, so never fear.

Then, I heard laughing and clapping. *A drug deal jingle. Seriously?* I thought. It was too bad what was being sold was illegal. Otherwise, it would have made a great commercial for advertisement. I must admit, I did enjoy it a little. The man singing sounded fun and he had a great voice. Maybe he had chosen the wrong path in life, or maybe he knew selling drugs was more profitable than working as a starving musician. He had obviously taken a risk by going down the wrong path. I had once overheard an adult say, "A life without risk, is like no life at all."

The next thing I felt were my dad's hands under my underarms again, lifting me up and over his head and back down. I was airborne for a second and then felt the cold, sticky ground under my bare feet. We were then in the elevator again, going down. *Wow! those guys are good!* I thought. *I'd never know there was a drug deal going on, if I didn't actually know.* I knew if I was ever questioned in Court, all I could say was, there was a man singing and I couldn't see anything, because I was playing a game that required me to wear a blindfold. The judge would be disappointed they couldn't prove my parents had brought me to a place that wasn't suitable for a child. After all, I could only describe an apartment with singing, if I told the partial truth. I tended to make things up a lot as a child. I still tend to make things up as an adult, as well. But, there was partial truth to all the stories I told as a child, which made them somewhat believable. As I would tell a story I would think, *Do they believe me, like 'Ripley's Believe It or Not'?* Even if someone didn't believe me, it was fun to exaggerate. I would watch their faces as I told a story, and it was rare for anyone to accuse me of lying, since parts of the stories were true. I had great respect for anyone who pointed out the bullshit parts of my stories, and I still do. To me, that's a turn-on. I love people who call things as they see them, without holding back; people who have the courage to look me straight in the eye, and tell me I'm full of shit. I want more people like them in my life. I hope to marry someone like that one day, because I would admire the fact they don't listen to nonsense. If I find someone like that when I'm older, I will consider myself blessed and lucky.

The elevator stopped to pick up three people. My folks didn't seem to care; not even one sigh or impatient rolling of their eyes. They even nodded, greeting the strangers as they entered the elevator. My parents were happy campers. They had gotten what they came for, sort of fast, regardless of the screaming match. The moment my dad had closed the door as we left, the fight in apartment 227 had picked up where it left off.

It was then back to the windowless back of the van, for the hour or so drive back. My mother let me sit on her lap in the front seat. Back then, in 1977, seat belts weren't yet required by law, cellphones didn't exist, and there was no such thing as Caller ID or even touch-tone phones. We had a rotary phone mounted up on the wall, and I had to stand on a chair to answer it. I wasn't really supposed to answer the phone, but I did it anyway. I would always answer it, whenever my mother took off and left me home alone for hours. 1977 was a year when you barely heard of child protective services, a year where hitting a defenseless child with a belt, because they had been disrespectful, was considered normal. There was discipline.

As we pulled up to park in front of the place where I slept and ate and stuff, *Mrs. Robinson*, the Simon and Garfunkel song, came on the radio. I loved that song and asked if we could hear the rest of the song before we went inside. The answer was 'no'. They didn't give me a reason, but I knew. They had a lot to do, like making sure their needles were clean. They had to separate the drugs into seven equal amounts, so they could be high every night of the upcoming week. They had to remember to bring out their favorite appliance, the drug scale with the chart.

I find it funny now, how they were so organized when it came to their drugs, but they couldn't ever seem to remember to take me in for a physical so I could start school on time. I missed the first two weeks of kindergarten due to their carelessness. Since I was the only kid who didn't get to meet my classmates on the first day of school, I felt like an outsider. Once I finally started school, I woke myself up each morning, ate chocolate donuts for breakfast, and would attempt to pour myself a glass of milk without spilling it from the heavy gallon jug. I would then get myself dressed, after I cleaned up the spilled milk.

I lived in Union City, New Jersey, on Kennedy Boulevard. Almost all our neighbors spoke only Spanish. Only a few spoke English. Union City wasn't the safest of places to live, because there was a lot of crime. For example, one day I was riding my big wheel. A tall man with red hair, an orange beard and creepy brown eyes blocked my path, causing me to stop pedaling. He asked me if I wanted a kitten. I told him no thanks, and started to pedal away, leaving him behind. I knew talking to strangers was forbidden, but how great would it be to have a kitten! A kitten would help conquer my boredom and loneliness. I knew my parents would most likely not allow me to keep it, but I wanted to at least see the kitten. So, I turned my big wheel around and pedaled back toward him. I caught up to him, looked up and said, "Mister, I changed my mind. Where is the kitten, sir?"

"Oh, you mean 'Whiskers'? Follow me, kid," he said. So, I did. I had to pedal really fast to keep up with his pace. The man sure did walk quickly. I followed him to a mausoleum. Behind the mausoleum were woods. The strange-looking man said I would have to walk from there, leaving my big wheel behind. He said the kitten was in the woods. I was skeptical, because I didn't want anyone to steal my big wheel. But, I followed anyway, walking behind him. We followed a long trail and then walked down a steep hill. When we arrived at the bottom of the hill, there was a man-made underground fort. It must have been ten feet deep. I followed him down dirt stairs. There was a couch, a wooden coffee table and even a TV! I had never known electricity could work outdoors and underground. In 1977, there were only thirteen channels, and you had to adjust the antenna on your TV to get better reception. I was amazed to know it was possible to watch TV outdoors. I enjoyed learning at least one new thing, each day. Sadly, that day I was going to learn things a child my age should never know, at least not until their late teenage years. I looked around in amazement. I asked the strange, bearded man where Whiskers was.

"Oh," he replied. "She must have gotten away. If you sit right here on my lap like you do with Santa, she will certainly come back soon. Whiskers always finds her way back, especially if she's hungry or thirsty." I suddenly felt really afraid, because I didn't see any cat food or a water bowl. I knew something wasn't right, but I really wanted to believe there was a kitten. I already knew there was no such thing as Santa. As scared as I was, I walked over to him and sat on his lap. He smelled like he hadn't taking a bath in months. *Pew, gross!* I thought. He started playing with my long blonde hair and breathing into my ear, making moaning noises. I was confused.

"What are you doing?" I asked him. He ignored my question.

"It gets hot down here," he said. He took his shirt off and told me to do the same.

"It's okay. I'm not hot," I told him.

"Do it now, or you'll never see that kitten!" he said. The tone of his voice scared me, and I jumped up from his lap and ran for the dirt stairs. He grabbed my leg from behind, on the fourth stair, and pulled me back down. Then, he walked to the top of the stairs and slid a big piece of wood over the opening, so we were closed in. It was very dark and he lit a match. I hated the smell of him, and the sulfur. He lit a lantern with the match, which made it easier to see. He then walked toward another lantern and turned it on. It was very bright then. I tried to hide my tears, but it was obvious I was crying because snot was running from my nose. I wiped the snot on my shirt.

"Alright," he said. "We're going to try this again, and don't you fucking *dare* run this time!"

"Help!" I screamed as loud as I could. But, that only made things worse. I should have remembered, "be seen and not heard", as I had been taught, because he grabbed me by my long hair and threw me on the couch.

"Now take off your shirt," he said. I did as he said that time, out of fear. "No need to yell," he said. "No one will be able to hear you in the mid woods." His voice changed as he started moaning, while he played with my hair again. He started kissing my lips. His hands were all over me like an octopus. He placed my hand on his private area and rubbed it up and down. I started to feel his private part get hard. Tears were rolling down my face. It was then that I realized, 'Whiskers' the kitten didn't exist. I was scared about what was going to happen next. I pretty much knew what he would do to me, because once when my parents thought I was sound asleep, they had watched a porno movie on a VHS tape. I had snuck several peeks out of curiosity.

The smelly man sat up, unbuckled his dirty jeans and pulled down his underwear. "I have to go home now," I cried out. That was the first time I had referred to my house as *home*. Bad things happened there, but at least I was always safe. My folks did drugs, but they wouldn't have ever allowed a stranger to hurt me, especially to take away my virginity. My dad once punched a man out for pushing me and laughing when I fell, so I felt protected when I was with my dad. The smelly man stood closely in front of me and told me I could go home if I did what he told me to do. *What if I say no?* I thought. *What will he do?* I didn't want to find out. "Okay", I said softly. "I'll do what you say."

"When I tell you to do something, you say 'yes' loudly. Then, you say 'sir'," he said. "You understand?"

"Oh-tay sir." I said. I used 'tay' in the hopes that if he heard innocence in my voice, he would let me leave. I was mistaken. My light, pretty blue eyes didn't help either. I was silently praying to *my* God for help. I always referred to the man upstairs as "*my* God" because it's *my* faith. He's *my* father. I wanted him all to *my*self. Everyone else could have their God, but *my* God was for me and only *me*. I tried not to treat *my* God as some genie granting me wishes, but I sometimes did.

"Sir?" I said softly.

"What?" he answered. I tried to hold back my tears.

"I know what you're going to do, because I saw it on TV. I can make it more pleasurable for you if I'm not so hot and sweaty. Do you think you can slide the wood roof off a little, to let some air in? I have asthma and I won't run this time. Promise." Surprisingly, he agreed. Maybe he wasn't as evil as I thought. Or, perhaps he was hot too. I don't know why I asked him to do that. The words just came out. I didn't even know what asthma was. Maybe *my* God made me ask.

"Make sure you are completely naked by the time I come back," he said. "Get naked. That will cool you off." No. I had been mistaken. He was evil. "Hurry up, Buttercup!" he continued. I took off all my clothes. When he came back, I asked him how he knew my nickname was 'Buttercup'. It was my CB radio handle. He said he knew everything about me, including where I lived, and my entire family.

"How come you don't look familiar to me, sir?" I asked. At the age of five, I somehow knew a lot of three-syllable words. I was an advanced speller, and knew the word "familiar" had the word "liar" in it. I also knew I probably wouldn't believe his answer.

"Because, you were blindfolded," he said. "If you tell anyone about this, I will kill your whole family. No more questions. Get down on your knees, you little bitch." I kneeled, like I did when I prayed before bedtime. "Good girl, Buttercup," he moaned. I felt even more scared then, knowing he knew where I lived, and knowing if I told on him, he could find me. The feelings I had inside were beyond horrific. There must have been a seven-syllable word for it, but I wasn't advanced enough in my spelling yet.

He took off his underwear and we were both completely naked, except for our socks. It wasn't the first time I had seen a penis, because of the porno I had watched that one time. But, it was the first time I had seen one in person. I took a deep breath, thinking about where I knew he would eventually put it. *Where is my God? I need him now!* I thought. *This can't wait. It's very time-sensitive!* The evil, smelly man started telling me how beautiful and lucky I was, that I was going to experience something only a few girls in my school had felt. I wondered who, but I didn't dare ask.

"No more questions," he said. "This is your lucky day, and it's going to feel better than being first in line at Disney World for your favorite ride. Relax. It's going to be magical." *Magical? Seriously?* That wasn't the word I would use to describe my emotions right then. *More like, terrifying beyond belief!* I thought. *Like going to the scariest haunted house.*

He kissed my neck. He looked into my eyes. He was kissing my neck and lips. He said to open my mouth and put my tongue into his mouth. He said to move my tongue around and around. His moaning got louder. He then threw me onto the couch. He said to spread my legs as if I was going to do a split. "No!" I screamed.

"Don't you ever say 'no' to me ever again, Buttercup, or I will make you watch me kill your whole family, and then I will slowly kill you!" he said. "Now I am soft," he continued. "Open your mouth wide and suck my cock. Bob your head, like when you bob for apples. Lick the sides, and then suck it like a pacifier or a lollipop." His voice was loud and extremely demanding. "Make sure you make it nice and wet, like you are washing it with your tongue." I did what he said. "Atta girl," he said, as I felt his penis get larger in my mouth. "Yeah, baby. Keep doing that and I will give you *two* kittens." But, I didn't even want one kitten anymore. I suddenly hated kittens. I just wanted to be back at my house, in a big, bad way.

"I'm ready to make love to you now, sweet girl," he said. *Love*, I thought. *It's more like, what you're about to do is going to ruin me forever, if you choose to let me live afterward.* This time, I wasn't blindfolded and something illegal was going to happen. He then laid me down on the couch, instead of throwing me. He laid down on top of me and I felt all his weight on my chest. As he was trying to find my private hole, I somehow squirmed away and ran for the dirt stairs again. I didn't get far though. He jerked me back by my hair so extremely hard, I was lifted off the floor a few feet. *This is nothing like a Disney World ride,* I thought. Since I had stopped him, his penis was soft again, so he shoved it into my tiny mouth. I thought about biting it, hard, but I was too afraid. He attempted to put his penis into my ass as a punishment. But, he had trouble getting it in because it had gone soft again. Every time I would try to run, it would distract him and I would have to work harder to make his penis hard again. *Why is this happening to me? Doesn't* my *God hear my prayers during this nightmare? How could* my *God allow any of this to happen?*

He made me suck his penis again, for the third time, saying first. "Three strikes and you're out. Do it right this time, or you will *never* see your family again." I remembered a time when I never even wanted to see my family again, but right then, I wanted to see my folks more than anything in the whole world. So I sucked it like a pacifier. I didn't want it to get hard again, but sadly, it did. Really hard. He turned me around. "I am going to fuck the shit out of you now," he said. "I love you, Buttercup!" He had trouble getting it into my ass, so he flipped me over and shoved it into my vagina, hard and fast. I screamed like I had never screamed before. It hurt so badly. It hurt more than when I had fallen out of the tree I had climbed when I was four, breaking both an arm and one of my legs. It hurt more than any spanking I had ever gotten, times a hundred.

After about twenty minutes of him humping pain into my little body, he screamed. "Oh God! I'm gonna cum inside of you now!" He made a loud sound, and looked as if he was being electrocuted. He then slowly pulled his penis out of me and smiled, showing his missing teeth. I held back my tears, but felt pain and emptiness inside. He then got up and grabbed a small suitcase from behind the couch. Inside was baby oil, charcoal, water, a metal container, cotton balls, matches, black powder, a credit card, a toothpaste cap, and tiny needles. I had no idea what he was planning to do until he said, "I keep my word. I am going to give you a kitten: a tattoo kitten on your ass. It will read 'Whiskers', so you don't forget her name. I need the practice, in case I go back to jail. I'm real good at jail tats. It pays well, and I need the practice. Now, hand me your underwear. Those are my souvenir to remember you, and this tattoo will be what you have to always remember me."

"My parents won't even allow me to get my ears pierced," I said. "I won't forget you ever, sir. Is it okay if you just keep my underwear only? I won't forget you or Whiskers."

"No," he said. "Don't you listen? I need the practice. Now turn around." I couldn't see what he was doing on my backside, but it didn't hurt as bad as the sex. About an hour later, he announced he was done. "You now have Whiskers," he said. "Such a cute kitten on your tiny ass, forever. This is the best tattoo I've ever done!" He then took out a Polaroid camera and snapped a picture of it. "Turn around and blow me a kiss," he said. "I want a picture of that as well." I did whatever he said. *This guy is beyond crazy*, I thought. I was hurting, and very scared he wouldn't ever let me leave. He kept taking pictures of me, making me smile. He made me do a bunch of poses naked. He then had a confused look.

"What is that buzzing noise?" he asked. I looked up and took a step. I could barely walk when I saw about two hundred bees come pouring in through the opening in the wood roof at the top of the stairs, the opening he had created when I had requested some fresh air because of my "asthma". Every single bee bypassed me and went straight for his penis, and the sweaty, smelly balls he had made me lick. *My* God had heard my prayers! I wondered why he was late, though I knew better than to ever question the motives of the

Creator of all things, including bees. The bees went to town, as if a gallon of honey had been poured onto his private area. And even though I couldn't run, I made a run for it. I was in a lot of pain, so I was in no rush. I knew those bees were my guardian angels. I had plenty of time to get back to my big wheel. *I need a doctor*, I thought as I slowly walked up the big hill, following the dirt trail and trying to avoid any poison ivy. I finally saw my big wheel. I tried to sit on it to ride it back to my house, but it hurt too much to sit. I decided to leave it there and walk. I was calling it a 'house' again, instead of a 'home', because my folks hadn't been around to protect me from the Evil Bearded Bee Man. I had to blame somebody else for not following the "no talking to strangers" rule. Since I was only five years old, I had to point the finger.

That's what kids do.

2 THE ARREST

I finally arrived at my house. The door was unlocked, but no one was home. "Hello!" I yelled out, but no one answered. I sat on the couch, turned on the TV and watched the cartoon, *Tom and Jerry*. I wondered where my folks were. Maybe they were sleeping? As I was still feeling pain with every single step I took, I slowly walked to my parents' room. My mother was sleeping. There was a needle in the center of her arm. Did she overdose again, or just fall asleep? I put my hand over her nose. She was breathing. I slowly took the needle out of her arm and then went back to the couch, to continue watching Saturday morning cartoons. I thought about calling the police, but I knew if they came and saw all the drugs and needles, it would be bad. I had had enough drama for one day, so I simply decided to let her sleep it off. Maybe my dad would come home so I could tell him what had happened. I was scared the Evil Bearded Bee Man would kill us if I told. That's the name I had decided to call him: The Evil Bearded Bee Man. I thought he was lying, especially since it would be hard to kill an entire family after getting multiple bee stings. *I'll have my dad call the police, since my mother is probably good for nothing today,* I thought. *Or, maybe I should keep this to myself since the Evil Bearded Bee Man can probably get someone else to kill us, if I tattle?*

I didn't know what to do. So, I just kept watching cartoons to keep my mind off it. It wasn't working though, because of the pain. It was safe to say, I liked bees much more than kittens. *My* God made sure I didn't even get one bee sting. *This day was certainly life-changing for me. I'm not sure if I'll ever be the same again. I wonder what condition the Evil Bearded Bee Man is in now? I'd better call the police.* I waited for another commercial and then got a chair, stood on it and dialed 9-1-1.

"9-1-1. What's your emergency?" A voice on the other line said. I replied, and told the voice there was a man in the woods, behind the mausoleum. I told them to go down the hill and they would see an underground fort.

"He needs medical attention." I said. "He got attacked by bees. Please hurry." The dispatcher said they would send an ambulance out and then asked me for my name. I hung up the phone. I didn't want the Evil Bearded Bee Man to die, but I wasn't ready to talk about it. I knew if or when I was ready to chat, at least I would have proof, because all 9-1-1 calls were recorded. I was happy with my choice to hang up. I also knew people usually thought kids made crank calls. However, when it came to 9-1-1, they were required to respond. Also, if the cops had come to my house to verify, I knew I would end up seeing my folks go directly to jail - without passing Go, or collecting $200 - for their bad "medicine" habit. I hoped the Evil Bearded Bee Man was in as much pain as me, if not more. But, I also didn't want him to be treated like a victim. I was the victim, not him. I needed to tell somebody soon. I also needed the physical and mental pain I felt to go away. I was so confused and wanted to protect my dysfunctional family. So, I decided to wait until my dad got home to speak up. That would give him time to get rid of all the drugs, or at least hide them well. I was thankful they only had a one-day supply left, because I was sure they would both want to get as high as possible after I told them. If there had been a seven-day supply left, both would probably overdose. They tended to go overboard when facing stress. *Today must be the day to break my silence. I need patience,* I thought. *My dad will be here soon. My mother should wake up at any minute now, at least I hope so.* Every minute felt like an hour. I was hungry, but too upset to eat. I wanted medicine, but not grown up medicine. Or, did I? I was willing to do anything to get rid of the pain. Plus, my body could most likely handle it since my mother did drugs throughout her whole nine months of me being in her tummy. I decided to wake my mother up from her sleep. I would rather tell her when she wasn't high, and she shouldn't be when first waking up. Sleep usually made it go away, and her words wouldn't be so slurred. My patience ran out, as I do not wait well. I slowly walked into her room. I tapped her on the shoulder and said, "Mother, please wake up." I shook her a few times and again said,

"Mother. Wake up." She turned to the right, away from me, hugging her pillow. "Mother? Mother! Wake up! Please!" I yelled. "I need to tell you something!"

"What!" she screamed.

"Call Dad and tell him to come home," I said. "I need to tell you both something, at the same time, so I don't have to tell the story twice." I knew I would have to tell the story twice, once the police got involved. But, she didn't need to know that right then.

"Tell us later. I'm sleeping!" she replied.

"No! Now! Wake up *now!*" I said loudly. I had never been so demanding in my life, so she sat up and looked at me.

"What is it?" she asked.

"Call Dad now, please. This can't wait," I said.

"Okay," my mother said as she reached for her glasses. "I'll try to reach him at work, but this better be good." Her bloodshot eyes started to open a bit wider. She looked at me as she stood up, rolled her eyes and then walked into the kitchen. She saw the chair I had forgotten to put back, near the phone. "Who did you call? You know you're not allowed to use the phone."

"The police," I said. Her bloodshot eyes opened wider than ever.

"What? Wait, what? Why? Are they coming here?"

"Relax, Mother," I said. "They aren't coming here. I had to report something. Please call Dad now."

"Fine," she said. "Get your hands out of your pants! You know better!" *I know better*, I thought. *Wow, what a hypocrite.* She always did so many things she knew she shouldn't do. But, whatever. I just wanted to say what needed to be said. The phone line was busy. My dad worked at New Jersey Bell, and it was taking forever to get through to him.

"Call his beeper and put in 9-1-1," I said to my mother.

"9-1-1 is for emergencies only," she said, as if I was unaware of that. It was then, my mother noticed my hands were still down my pants and tears were in my eyes. I rarely cried. Surprisingly, instead of yelling at me again, she asked calmly, "Are you okay? Why are you crying?" I pulled down my pants and she saw the blood and scratches. "Oh, God," she said. "I am going to run you a bath and see what we are dealing with here. Please tell me what happened. Did you fall?"

"I will tell you and Dad together," I said. I went into the bath, as we waited for Dad to call back or come home. My mother noticed the tattoo.

"Who--? What--?" She couldn't even finish her sentence. She finally caught her breath. It took a few minutes. "I need to take you to a hospital," she finally said. "Can you wait for Dad, since he has the van, or should I call an ambulance?" I always seemed to be the one to make the adult decisions. I told her we could wait for Dad to come home. I could wait. She took me out of the bath, gave me some children's Tylenol and laid me on the couch. I was wearing my blue bathrobe. My other nickname was "Smurfette", because of the blue robe and my blond hair. She went to the freezer and retrieved an ice pack. "Put this where it hurts the most," she said as she handed it to me. I put it on my private part. "That's what I thought," she said, as I saw my mother cry for the first time, ever. She called my dad's beeper again. "Stay calm," she said to me. "Dad will come home soon, or he'll call. He's probably on a telephone pole right now, fixing wires. Stay strong, baby girl." She combed my hair with her fingers and said everything would be alright. "Tell me what happened," she said again.

"Please," I said. "I don't want to tell the story twice. Let's wait for Dad first, okay?"

"Okay," she said. Wow. I couldn't believe my mother's eyes were filled with tears. Maybe she was biologically programmed to love me. Or, maybe she cared a lot about me, because I don't know if she knew what love was. Then again, maybe she was crying because I ruined her plans for later. *She may have to wait to get high. Oh, the horror.* When it came to drugs, she liked to stay on schedule. I wanted the phone to ring, but me staring at it didn't make that happen. I ended up falling fast asleep on the couch, as I waited.

I awoke to my dad's voice. "Wake up. Wake up," he said. I slowly opened my eyes, trying to get them adjusted to the light. I wiped the sleepers out of both of my eyes with my knuckles. "What happened, Buttercup?" he asked. *Oh shit, fuck, sob,* I thought. It hadn't been a bad dream. I knew all the curse words from TV, and from the street, plus my folks' poker parties. I wouldn't have ever said them out loud. *A mean man hurt me in my private part where I go pee-pee. He also gave me a tattoo on my butt. I asked him not to,* I wanted to say. But, I started crying harder than I had ever cried before, and hugged my dad tighter than I had ever hugged anyone in my life. My dad asked what happened and I wimped out, for safety reasons. I said I didn't want to talk about it just yet. My dad carried me outside, where it was already dark out. I wondered how long I had been asleep. I was surprised the phone hadn't woken me up as it usually did. I just remembered falling asleep to the Flintstones. My mother, who was only wearing a bathrobe with long sleeves, got into the passenger side of the van that had no back windows. My dad placed me on the backseat on my belly. My mother put a band aid in the center of her arm. When I pulled out the needle it had bled a little.

"Where are we going, Dad?"

"To the hospital," he said as he drove very fast. A song by Meatloaf came on the radio, called *Two Out of Three Ain't Bad.* I thought the song lyrics were bullshit. If somebody wanted you and needed you, but would never love you, that made them a user. That would make anyone sad. *Two out of three ain't bad, it's horrible,* I thought. I was trying to think of anything but the pain, which seemed to be getting easier to deal with. "I don't understand why you won't talk to us about what happened to you, Buttercup," my dad said. "But, you must tell the doctors and nurses what happened, or they won't be able to make you feel better. Deal?"

"Deal," I agreed reluctantly. We arrived at the hospital and went straight to the ER waiting room. I quickly started running out of things to look at. There was a news program on the TV about the White House and Jimmy Carter. Boring. There was a child coughing every five minutes, an old man reading a magazine and a water fountain that barely worked. When I pushed the button, I had to lean all the way over and put my mouth on it for a tiny little sip. It was frustrating. There were doctors being paged over a loud speaker.

The seats were uncomfortable, and my feet didn't reach the floor, as always. I sat on my hands to help deal with the pain, since it was inappropriate to have my hands down my pants in a public place, or anywhere for that matter. Our paperwork had been done and handed in for over an hour, and they didn't appear to be busy, so I wondered why it was taking so long for them to call my name. Finally, twenty minutes later, a nurse came out and called my name. It felt the same way it did when I was really hungry and our food would finally come out, when we would sometimes go to a restaurant. The nurse took my blood pressure. It felt funny, like my arm was about to blow up. She was not a very nice nurse. Her name tag read, "Sam". I had never liked that name. She had the same name of a mean girl at school, who bullied me. The nurse even looked a bit like her. I could have sworn I saw Sam the mean girl walking by, as I was thinking about all of that. But, I suppose I wasn't thinking straight. It had been a rough, stressful day.

I stepped on the scale. After that, Sam the nurse wrote down my temperature and weight on my chart. Then, she said the doctor would be with me shortly, as she rushed out and shut the door. I looked around the room. Not much to see. There had been more to look at in the waiting room. I noticed some oversized cotton swabs and almost got up to take one. I don't know why I would have even wanted one, but I did. It would have hurt to stand up anyway, so I decided against getting up to explore. About twenty minutes later, which had felt like hours, the doctor finally came in. He was very tall and handsome. My neck started to hurt a bit, after looking so high up at him. After answering some standard questions, he asked me to take off my clothes and put on a gown with the open part in the back. I had trouble with the ties. It was a bit confusing for me, but I figured it out. I had plenty of time to, since the doctor took a long time to come back. Most doctors did that and I had always found that rude, as if their time was more important than mine. I sat at the end of the examination table. I had goosebumps because it was cold, and my backside was open because of the gown. The doctor came back in and introduced himself again, as if it was the first time we had met. Weird.

"Why are you here today?" he asked.

"I have pain where I go to the bathroom, when I go number one," I replied. "It stopped bleeding, though." The doctor had me lie down to have a look.

"The bleeding is caused from the hymen stretching. It won't bleed anymore now," he explained.

"What?" I asked.

"I know you don't know what that means. You're not supposed to, especially at your age," he said. I admit, I did like the fact he spoke to me like an adult. The doctor continued, "We'll run some tests to make sure you didn't get any infection or disease from receiving a tattoo from a dirty needle, along with other dirty things. I am going to have a female doctor run some more tests and prescribe some meds for you. Would you like to tell me what happened?"

"No, not really," I said. He said okay, and told me to get dressed.

"A lady from child protective services is going to come in later and ask you a few questions," he said. I knew where that was going. I didn't want anyone to think my parents had done this to me.

"Wait," I said. "Can I speak to the police instead?" The doctor said he would see what he could do, and left the room again. Before he closed the door, he stopped and turned back toward me.

"I almost forgot," he said, holding out a handful of different colored lollipops. "Pick a color." I chose green out of the five different colored lollipops, and he left. Next, a woman named Mrs. Wilkens came in. She was very pleasant, and held a rape kit in her hand. Over the next four hours, I was poked, prodded, swabbed and photographed on the place where my body had been violated. It was no picnic.

"Okay, the tests are done," the nurse finally said. "You were a brave little soldier. I'd like for you to rest a bit and then the police will come in and ask you a few questions."

"Can I see my parents first?" I asked her.

"I'm sorry," she said. "You can't see them until after you speak with the police. It is standard procedure." I closed my eyes and fell asleep. The medicine they gave me had made me drowsy. When I woke up about an hour later, two police officers were standing in front of the examination table.

They had waited for me to wake up on my own, instead of waking me up. I thought that was considerate. One of them asked me how I was feeling. I told them I was a little sore. They then informed me, the test results had proven I had been sexually assaulted, and asked me if I felt ready to answer some questions.

"We prefer to do it now, since it's fresh in your memory," one of the police officers explained. I asked if I could see my parents first. The answer was no. "You can see them when we're done with the interview," one of them said. So, I agreed to do the interview right away, since hadn't seen my family for hours. They had me get into a wheelchair, and did a few pop-a-wheelies, which hurt a little. But, they did make me laugh. They also swayed the wheelchair back and forth, fast, like I was on some sort of amusement park ride. I enjoyed it. When we arrived at a private conference room, there were three uniformed police officers and a social worker. A video camera and cassette tape recorder were both set up, too. One of them asked me to have a seat, and reminded me the interview would be recorded. They also said my parents had signed a consent form, giving their permission for the interview to be done. I was happy my family knew what was going on. One of the cops reminded me it was very important I tell the truth. He said they would find out the truth if I fibbed, so to please not make up stories. "This is very serious," he said. I told them I understood and would not fib. With that said, they started. Someone asked me what had happened that morning. I told them everything. I told them about the big wheel ride, getting offered a kitten, following the man into the woods. I described the underground fort, with the TV and the lanterns, and the dirt stairs and the piece of wood that he used like a roof. I explained he had threatened to kill me and my family if I tattled, and that I was scared for my own and my family's safety. That was why I hadn't been sure if I should tell anyone, I explained. I didn't want him to kill my family, like he said he would, if I tattled.

"You're doing the right thing. You're a brave little gal," one of the police officers said reassuringly. "Is there anything else you can remember?"

"Yes," I said. "He said a few girls in my school were also lucky enough to get to experience getting made love to, by him. I'm not sure which ones, because he told me to not talk anymore since I had tried to get away so many times."

"How did you finally get away?" the same cop asked.

"Oh, yeah," I said. "I'm sorry I forgot to tell you. A whole bunch of bees flew in and went straight toward his private part. I believe *my* God answered my silent prayers, and made that happen. I didn't even have to run to escape, thankfully, because I was in pain. But, I was able to walk. Not one bee came near me or stung me. It was as if the bees were on a mission." As I finished speaking, two of the cops immediately left the room, without saying a word. I found that odd. I continued, telling the officers still there, that he had also given me a tattoo, he had taken pictures of me, and that he had kept my underwear as a souvenir.

"Well, that's enough for today," the social worker said. "I will have your parents come in now. You were a tremendous help today, and don't be afraid of this man ever hurting you or your family. I promise you, you are all safe." I thanked her. When my parents came in, I gave them each a hug. We left the room, and picked up my paperwork and prescription from the front desk. We walked to the windowless van, got in and headed toward home. There was silence in the van. I was willing to talk, but it had been a long day. We were all tired and needed a good night's sleep. I knew we could all discuss it the next day. We stopped at the pharmacy on the way home, and we all went to bed shortly after. My mother and dad tucked me in together, which they hadn't done in years. It felt good. I asked them if I could have a puppy. They said maybe. To me, that was better than a 'no'. They read my favorite book to me, *There's a Monster at the End of This Book*. After that, they left the room. I lied awake thinking, and could hear them talking about doing drugs. But, I didn't care. *Whatever makes them happy,* I thought, *because they both took good care of me today.*

When I woke up, I needed my medicine. I walked toward my parents' room. I heard them talking but I couldn't hear what they were saying, so I got a glass and put the glass to the door with my ear on the glass. It was a trick I had been taught, to hear better through a wall. Their voices were still muffled, but I could make out most of what they were saying. They wanted to finish the drugs fast, and then buy a drink that would clear it out of their systems quickly, so they could pass a drug test. They said the social workers could arrive at any time, without any warning or appointment, to give them drug tests and see if everything was normal. Our family was far from normal. Maybe the social worker had been able to tell they did drugs, since their appearance made it so obvious. There was a chance the family would be torn apart, if they didn't stop doing drugs. I hadn't told the cops about how he knew my nickname, or about how he knew I was blindfolded, because I didn't want them questioning my parents about it. I hadn't told my parents that part of my horrific experience either. They had enough on their plates. Although they never physically hurt me, it was their job to make sure they were not deemed unfit parents. I heard footsteps, so I quickly tiptoed back to my room with the glass, so I wouldn't be caught eavesdropping. I waited twenty minutes and then knocked on their door. They said to come in. I asked for my medicine and they gave me chewable pills, with some water. *Today is just another TV day*, I thought. I wasn't ready to go back to school yet, so my mother took time off work to take care of me. She made me stop watching TV for an hour, so she could watch her soap opera, *Days of Our Lives*. When it was over she took a nap, so I changed the channel right as my brother appeared. He rarely came out of his bedroom. I rolled my eyes, because I knew he was going to change the channel as he always did. My brother and sister weren't at school, due to their school being closed for the day for a teacher's conference.

He sat down, draped his arm over me and asked, "What are we watching?" I automatically knew he knew, because he didn't take the remote away like he always did so rudely. I sighed.

"Who told you?" I asked.

"Dad and Mother," he answered. I told him we were watching *Scooby-Doo*. He asked me, "Where is that Scooby now?" I answered that he was hiding under the couch, because he was scared of the cat. Then, my brother started singing:

Scooby Dooby Doo, where are you? We got some work to do now.

I joined in and sang with him. It made me laugh.

Scooby Dooby Doo, where are you? We need some help from you now.

Come on Scooby-Doo, I see you. Pretending you got a shiver.

But you're not fooling me, 'cause I can see, the way you shake and shiver.

You know we got a mystery to solve, so Scooby-Doo be ready for your act. Don't hold back!

And Scooby-Doo, if you come through, you're going to have yourself a Scooby snack! That's a fact!

We were singing it so loudly and snapping our fingers. It was the most fun I had enjoyed with my brother in a long time. My sister came home, with the cheese and cracker packs with the little red stick in each one, to spread the cheese on the crackers. *Handisnacks!* Plus, a Slim Jim for me. My two favorite foods of all time! I looked at her.

"You know, too?" I asked.

"I know, too," she said, as she got teary-eyed. "Are you ready to talk about it?" she asked.

"No, not yet," I said. My brother stood up and clapped his hands.

"I'm ordering pizza!" he announced. Then, he pointed at me as he walked backward toward the phone, and said, "Extra cheese for you!" I felt excited because pizza was my third favorite food. My brother and sister set the table, and my parents finally came out of their room shortly after. They both looked as if they had been run over by a truck. My dad asked my brother if he had ordered soda, too. He said, "Yes, two bottles of Pepsi." Wow, a family dinner! All of us hadn't eaten together in years. Usually, we ate in separate rooms or in front of the TV. But that night, we were all eating at the living room table. I felt excited again.

I walked over to the couch, stood on it, and looked out the window to wait for the pizza guy. Every minute felt like an hour. *Will he ever get here?* It had only been three minutes and they probably hadn't even put it in the oven yet, but I was so anxious for it to arrive. Thirty-five minutes later it arrived. The delivery guy had forgotten the soda. *Ugh.* He apologized and said he would be right back with it. He came back fifteen minutes later, but to me that wasn't right. I didn't care though, because I was experiencing a family pizza dinner; a dysfunctional family pizza dinner, but it was my family. I loved them despite the craziness. They kept my mind off the Evil Bearded Bee Man. Much to my surprise, no one talked about what happened to me. They were waiting for me to talk, which was not going to happen anytime soon. I just wanted to forget about it. As I was eating the pizza, my dad folded it in half for me and I noticed I was getting a lot of attention. All eyes were on me, but I didn't give in. I didn't want to talk about it. I excused myself and asked if I could go to my room to sleep. My sister asked if I wanted a bubble bath first. "No, thanks," I answered. "I just want to sleep now. Is that okay?" Everybody answered, "That's okay" at the same time; in stereo. I never went to sleep as early as 6:47 p.m., but it had only been two days since the incident. I wanted to soak up the attention I rarely got from my family, but I was feeling physically and mentally exhausted. I figured the medicine was a big reason why I was so tired. I was in dreamland within a matter of minutes. The attention would have to wait. I slept longer than I had ever slept before. When I woke up early the next morning, it was twelve hours later. I couldn't remember any of my dreams, which was odd. I usually remembered at least one, but not that time. Dreams are funny like that.

I decided I wanted to go to school. The doctor had said I could go when I felt ready to. Most kids didn't like school, but I did. I hated rules, but I enjoyed being around children my own age; not children in adult bodies. The only part I didn't like about school was the bully, Sam. She would knock my books out of my hands, make me pay her a toll to walk up the stairs, plus tape "kick me" signs to the back of my shirt sometimes. *Perhaps today will be the day she picks the wrong kid to bully,* I thought. I knew I had a lot of pain and anger and I wouldn't be afraid to stick up for myself this time. She picked on me so much. Most kids would simply tell a teacher, but not me. I knew "snitches get stitches". I smelled bacon cooking, so I decided to get out of bed. I still love that smell. My mother was cooking? I looked out the window to see if pigs were flying, but I didn't see any. She had made me bacon, toast, and eggs that still had shells in them. But, I was impressed, and happy she was at least trying, even if she only had to because of the authorities. I felt proud of her. She could have made something simple, like oatmeal in the microwave or cold cereal, but she chose to go above and beyond. I pretended to enjoy the undercooked eggs and burnt toast. She asked me if I wanted to stay home for the day or go to school. I said I wanted to go to school. I was on a mission to stand up to that bully, for the first time ever. I decided this would be the day she would be taught a lesson for once. I even put a "kick me hard" sign in my backpack, for her back. I felt confident and strong, and I was looking forward to defending myself. I was going to "get her".

When I arrived at school, I looked for Sam but didn't see her anywhere. That was strange. She usually found me first, as bullies usually do. *Just great, I finally have the courage to stand up for myself and this is the one day she's not right here in my face. No fair.* The bell rang. When I walked into my classroom, I immediately noticed Sam's chair was empty. Oh, this was just perfect. The one time I was finally ready to stick up for myself and confront her, she's homesick. I could have been homesick as well. This girl had ruined my day without even bullying me. I found that so frustrating and disappointing. I could have been home watching TV and getting VIP treatment. All day long, I couldn't concentrate on whatever the teacher was trying to teach. It was as if I had a secret I wanted to tell, but at the same time I wanted to keep it to myself. At 3:00 p.m., the dismissal bell finally rang. When you stare at a clock, time goes so slowly.

I went straight home, ate a Slim Jim and some cheese and crackers and then started my homework. My mother was on the phone talking about somebody who was in the hospital. I just assumed she was discussing my hospital visit, but only heard part of the conversation. When she hung up the phone, she told me the father of my friend, Sam, was in the hospital. *Well, that explains why she wasn't in school today,* I thought. I asked why her dad was in the hospital.

"I'm not sure," my mother said. She explained she had been talking to Sam's mother, who had hung up because she had to answer the door. She was going to call my mother back. "Some of their family members don't even know yet, so I don't need you telling your friends at school," my mother said. It sounded serious. I didn't know why my mother thought Sam was my friend. Just because she and Dad partied with Sam's junkie parents didn't automatically make us friends. I never complained about Sam bullying me, because I knew nothing good would come from it. Sometimes, I would let her pick on me because I knew what it was like to live with parents who were junkies. I wasn't sure if Sam knew that I knew her parents partied at my house, but I never mentioned it to her. I didn't need her big mouth telling my classmates that my parents were junkies. Then…

Bam! It hit me like a ton of bricks. I *had* seen Sam at the hospital. I put two and two together. Her father must have been there because of all the bee stings, at the same time I had been there. That was why two of the cops had immediately left my interview when I had mentioned the bees. *My mother is lying,* I thought. She knew why Sam's dad was in the hospital. She had been on the phone for a long time with Sam's mom, so she must have told her. It was a no-brainer. My bully's dad raped me. Disney was right. It's a small world after all. I wondered if my mother really knew for sure. I knew she had read the police report, and the bees were mentioned in the report. Was she choosing one mistake in her life: drugs, over *me*, another mistake in her life? I liked Sam's mother. She partied, but she was a good soccer mom. I didn't believe in coincidences, but the Evil Bearded Bee Man had said he knew my family. I wondered if he had also raped Sam as well, since he mentioned he had also done it to some of my schoolmates. If he had raped her, I was pretty sure her mom didn't know. Sam's mom was kind, reliable and very protective of Sam. I wouldn't have minded if my parents had hung out with her socially, but her husband was another story. She had definitely chosen the wrong guy to marry. I wondered if she knew what he was doing, or if she was in the dark. Or… Maybe, she knew he was accused of it, but believed her husband was innocent. So many unanswered questions. They were starting to give me a headache. I decided to count sheep again until I fell asleep. The next day, I was going to request another family meeting along with police and detectives, if possible.

The next morning, my mother made pancakes. I was happy she was trying to better herself. At the breakfast table, I requested another family meeting with the detective there. I said, "Ask me no questions and I will tell you no lies." They asked anyway. I said, "Please respect my wishes and make this happen." They agreed.

My dad said, "I will call today and try to set it up for 6:00 p.m. tomorrow. Deal?"

"Deal," I said. I thanked my mom for the pancakes. They hadn't been cooked all the way, but at least she had tried. *I think she needs a cooking lesson*, I thought. *I pray she doesn't attempt to make chicken.* I got ready for school, wondering if Sam would be there that day. My feelings had changed for her, since I had realized we may have so many depressing things in common. I wondered if the reason Sam picked on me was her father's fault. Maybe she was one of the children he had spoken about raping. *Maybe he lives a double, possibly triple life, where he is well-respected but has many dirty secrets,* I thought. I believed all his victims were afraid to speak up, and *my* God had chosen me to put an end to his horrific crimes. My experience with him had been horrible, but maybe my speaking up would help others break their silence. I was more concerned about the girls too afraid to speak up, no matter what. Perhaps it had occurred multiple times to the same children; maybe even my classmates. I felt like it was my job to put an end to it, once and for all. That was my mission. *My* God wanted me to do this. I could feel it, as if I was 'the chosen one'. To me, the bees were proof.

The next day at school, I didn't hand in my homework. My teacher didn't seem to care, because it was the first time it had ever happened. Plus, it was only kindergarten. I noticed Sam was nowhere to be seen. The teacher had an announcement to make, so she clapped her hands five times. Whenever she clapped her hands five times in a certain rhythm, all the kids in the class would clap back the same way, and that meant we would all stay quiet after the clapping was finished. The teacher started to speak. "I want to tell all of you, the reason Sam hasn't been in school is because her father is in the hospital. Sadly, he was trying to get rid of a beehive and ended up getting stung by many, many bees. Unfortunately, he is allergic to bees. It is not mandatory, but as a nice gesture, I would like you all to make get-well cards for Sam's dad. Please raise your hand if this is something you would like to do for Sam and her dad, during this difficult time." As some of the kids raised their hands, I looked around the room. Out of twenty-six students, only eleven had raised their hands. I was one of them. The teacher looked confused, because the entire class usually always enjoyed making cards for people. She told the class, anyone not making a card could read, start on that day's homework, play quietly with the toys in the corner, or draw on the blackboard. They all chose to draw on the blackboard, all girls. I could tell the teacher couldn't figure out why most of them didn't want to make a card instead. Maybe she thought it was because Sam wasn't the nicest kid, so some of the other kids didn't care about her father being in the hospital. The teacher handed out construction paper, crayons, and an envelope to me and the other ten of my classmates who had volunteered to make cards. I wrote down the names of the girls who wanted no part of it, in my notebook. Ironically, out of all the colors to choose from, the teacher gave me a yellow piece of paper. Yellow: the same color as bees. I drew a picture of a mausoleum, with woods behind it and a steep hill. I then drew a picture of an underground fort. I drew as many bees as would fit on the paper, all flying around his private area. On the other folded side of the card, I drew a court room, a picture of him handcuffed, and a jail cell. I wrote: "Get well soon, so my tattooed kitten ass can see your sorry ass in Court. You took a lot away from me, but I will never give you the power to make me keep your illegal secrets. You're busted!"

I sealed it, so the teacher couldn't see it. On the front of the envelope, I drew a picture of a tattooed kitten and wrote next to it: "Sam, please open this with your dad. I can't wait until he's better. Love, Buttercup." The teacher silently read the outside of the envelope, and gave me a surprised look with a wink. She knew Sam bullied me, even though I never tattled on her. "Great drawing of a kitten," she said. I looked around at what the other kids' cards looked like. They had drawn rainbows and hearts and had written get-well wishes. The girls who had chosen to draw on the blackboard instead, their moods were changed for the rest of the day. They looked as if they had relived an experience they would rather forget. I knew why, but the teacher was clueless. I knew in my gut that I had found more rape victims. It was hard to not say anything, but I kept it to myself. I knew the Evil Bearded Bee Man was in bad shape. I didn't wish him well, but I also didn't wish him dead. The Bible says to never wish anyone dead, and I, along with others, deserved justice. *My* God had chosen me to make sure this wouldn't happen again, and I would try my best to not let Him down. *My* God had given me the courage and strength to make sure the Evil Bearded Bee Man would get what he deserved. I was not afraid to confront him. I was looking forward to it, and I decided I would convince my classmates to look forward to it, as well. If they said "no" at first, no worries. In time, I knew they would follow my lead. When *my* God wanted something, he made it happen, and nothing in the Universe would get in the way. The anticipation of not knowing the outcome, not knowing if there would even be a trial, gave me anxiety. I decided to pray for patience. I had a lot of classmates to convince to speak up: ten, or fifteen, or maybe even more. I had a lot of talking, plus convincing to do. But, it was nothing I couldn't handle. *My* God had chosen me.

3 THE MEDIA

It was finally 3:00 p.m. and I needed to think about what I would say at the 6:00 p.m. meeting, if my dad had been able to set it up. I also needed to find out the Evil Bearded Bee Man's status. I had so many unanswered questions, but I was on a mission. When I was on a mission, I was inpatient, annoying and persistent. I'm still that way. I will get answers, even if it takes longer than I anticipate. I am determined to get answers, and I make sure things get done.

After school, I did my normal routine: ate my cheese and crackers pack and a *Slim Jim*, plus watched *The Jetsons* cartoon alone. I pretended my brother was there singing along with me, like he had done when we watched *Scooby-Doo*. But, he was at basketball practice and my sister was at cheerleading practice. My parents were at work, so as I had been told, I locked the door and deadbolted it until they got home. I wasn't allowed to answer the door or use the phone, unless someone used the secret code, since my mother couldn't afford to miss any more work. The secret phone code was, the phone would ring only once, to give me time to drag over a chair, and get up on it to reach the phone to answer it. Then, it would ring again only twice. I had to wait. I was only allowed to answer it the third time it rang, and only after the fourth ring. Dumb rules, but they were trying to keep me safe. If I was in the bathroom, the phone didn't get answered. I didn't like rules and except for school, it was rare that I followed them. I know that's not a very good trait, but it's the way I've always been, even as an adult. It's a bit more under control now, though.

It was 4:00 p.m. when I realized I had two hours left until I would be telling the police and my parents, who I believed had raped me. I knew exactly what I was going to say, but didn't know how my dad or mother was going to react. I looked at the clock. Now, I had 119 minutes until I found out. I felt sleepy again from the meds, so I took a nap on the couch as I waited. I woke up to a knock on the door. My dad answered the door and it was a cop and a detective. My mother offered them something to drink. They both declined.

"Please sit down," my dad said. The five of us sat at the kitchen table: me, my dad, my mother, the detective and the cop. The detective asked me how I was feeling.

"Better. Thanks," I answered. But, that was a lie. He then asked me what was on my mind. I stuttered a little bit, "I'm pretty sure I know who did those bad things to me. I'm almost positive it was Sam Gonzalez's father." My mother stood up and raised her voice, upset, saying I shouldn't falsely accuse people. "I wouldn't accuse anyone if I didn't have a good reason to, Mother." I said. *What's wrong, Mother? Are you afraid if it's true, you could lose your drug connection? Why else would she protect him?* I wondered. I stood up and looked at the detective. "I found out at school that Sam's dad is in the hospital due to bee stings. The only reason I got away is because the bees went after him. I don't know what else he would have done to me if I hadn't gotten away." My mother's stare caught my attention for a moment. *Is that suspicion on her face?* I looked back at the detective, and then my dad as I continued. "Read my statement or watch the video of my interview with the cops, if you don't believe me. There should also be a tape of my 9-1-1 call, explaining where he was. Those bees saved me."

"And, yet you didn't get one bee sting?" my mother said, looking me up and down. *Whose side are you on?* I wondered.

"No, Mother; not that you can see," I said. "But, I did get a sting somewhere else and it still hurts." That shut her up. She looked at the floor as I continued. "Sam's dad was in the hospital the same day I was being treated." *You think that was a coincidence, Mother?* I tried my best to use four-syllable words when I wanted to be heard and not just seen. "Can you verify that, detective?"

"Yes, young deputy," he answered, nodding. "You are on the right track. The man you are accusing is handcuffed to his hospital bed." My mother's jaw dropped. "It's in the statement you gave us, but he claims he has no memory of what happened." *Liar,* I thought. The detective continued. "We don't have a statement, because he can't speak due to his lips and tongue being too swollen, and he refuses to write a statement. The bees really did a number on him, and it's amazing he's still alive. He's requested a lawyer, but the lab results will speak for themselves. It will take a few weeks for the DNA to be processed. Allow us to do our jobs, okay? Everybody is innocent until proven guilty."

"Okay," I agreed. "But, I believe he also hurt some other girls in my class. I think they're too scared to say anything. His threats of killing our families and pets… I know I almost didn't tell." The detective nodded, listening carefully as I continued. "I think I know exactly which girls he could have raped. The teacher asked us to make get-well cards for him, but a lot of girls didn't want to." The detective handed me a miniature version of a police badge. Cool.

"Good work, but just let the police department handle this for now. Please keep quiet for now, and don't speak about this to anyone at all, except your guidance counselor at school. I'd like for you to talk to her, especially if you feel like you need to." I agreed, and watched as the detective pulled out a book and put it on the table in front of me. He opened it, and I saw it was full of mug shots of a few dozen men. The detective went through it with me, turning each page, waiting to see if I recognized the man who had attacked me. I didn't see a mug shot of him.

"I don't see him," I said, shaking my head. "None of these guys are him."

"Okay, that's fine," said the detective reassuringly. "We just needed to have you look at these photos as part of our procedure." The detective closed the book and picked it up. He glanced at the cop and nodded. They both started to stand up. "I will keep you all posted, okay?" The detective said. "Just so you are aware, we have found some hard evidence against him, inside his underground fort. Once again, it's going to take time and patience for us to build a case against him." I noticed my mother was still staring at the floor. I wondered what she was thinking, but I quickly pushed the thought aside as I continued to listen to the detective. "But, pictures don't lie," he continued. "We have found plenty of evidence to put him away for a very long time. He actually made it easy for us." *Oh, I wonder if he took pictures of the other girls too?* I thought. *Bet he did.* The detective looked at me again. "You're very brave, and you're doing a really good job helping us. I want to repeat, building a case against him may take weeks or even months, okay? But, you stay strong. Just let us do our jobs." I nodded in agreement. "Please don't talk to *anyone* about this, folks," he reminded my parents, as he shifted his attention back to the two of them.

Dad agreed, "Yes, yes. Of course, we won't talk to anyone about this." My mother looked up just long enough to respond to him with a nod. The detective focused on me again.

"It's important to not talk about this with *any* of your classmates, especially since you think he may have hurt some of them too. Okay?" I nodded as he continued. "Sometimes, like in the game 'telephone'—"

"Oh!" I interrupted. "I love that game! It's when you whisper something to each other, one after the other, and what the first person said - it's always different at the end." It was a fun game. The detective smiled and nodded.

"Yes, that's right," he said. "So, you know whatever you say to anyone else could be misunderstood, and it could turn into untrue gossip. We can't let that happen, because this is a *very* sensitive issue. That's why you need to keep this to yourself." I agreed, and he pointed at me and smiled. "You, my mini deputy, I want you to speak to your guidance counselor at school at least twice a week." He reached out and shook my hand, and then turned to my parents, extending his hand. The cop shook my hand as the detective said to my parents,

"Also, tell your son and other daughter to please not speak about this to anyone. The police department is required by law to release information about the community, to the media. So, you'll see our public information officer make a statement soon. The police like to keep things private as the media tends to exaggerate. It's been an ongoing and controversial struggle for years, and will probably never get resolved. I can't force you to stay away from the media or talk shows. It's your choice. Most people do it for the money. In my experience, the longer you keep silent, the more they will pay you later, due to the suspense. The other parents and girls may decide to go public, but the media always wants to go to the original victim first. Try your best to take my advice. You may regret it if you don't. It is good advice." The detective turned to the cop. "Do you have anything?"

"We will keep you informed," the cop said, looking at me and then my parents. "Please feel free to contact us anytime. This case is top priority." Then, he handed me a bag with a bulletproof vest inside. I looked inside and noticed the card I had made in class was tucked into the bag too. I looked at the detective, and he put his index finger over his mouth like a hush sign, and winked at me.

"I request you wear this at all times," the cop said to me. "Even at bedtime. The FBI is also investigating this case and needs you all safe from possible home invasion." He then handed my dad a bag, with four more bulletproof vests inside.

"I recommend the whole family wear these at all times," the cop said. "He is the leader of a mob. Police officers will be watching your house at all times, for your protection. The vests are uncomfortable, but they could save your lives. I'm not trying to scare you, but if any of you get shot in the chest, you must play dead. There are other victims who have come forward already, thanks to you Laura." He nodded at me and smiled. "And, since it made it to the news, they were told to do the same thing. They will always be wearing one under their clothing as well."

I liked this cop. He had kept my evil card a secret. "Although this man will be in prison after he's released from the hospital, he is part of a dangerous mob. He may have friends who will want to injure you all, so you will be unable to testify in Court, and because you have spoken up. This story is big, since so many young girls were raped," the cop said. "Please have patience as we gather facts together, plus test results. You do have the right to know that what happened to your daughter also happened to over twenty-five other girls her age. Your brave daughter is the first one who came forward. Other children are now speaking up, but please don't believe everything you hear on the TV. Media tends to exaggerate, for sales and acknowledgement. It's best if you come and go through your basement door, until this calm down. If you ever feel you need a police escort or help in any way, then contact us. Unfortunately, the media does have the right to stand outside your home. In fact, they're out there right now. News travels fast. They are allowed on the street and sidewalk, but not on your property. I can have them arrested for trespassing, if that occurs. We are only a phone call away. Sometimes, a mob person pretends to be a news reporter, so be extra careful. There will also be security at your front and back doors, twenty-four hours a day for your protection, thanks to the FBI."

I was relieved they were looking out for our safety, but I hated not being allowed to talk to my friends about it. I guess cops could even control what you could or couldn't say. That didn't seem fair. Children talked to other children better than they talked to adults. But, I was going to try and play by the rules. "It's not against the law to tell your story to reporters, but it certainly will not help your case," the cop said. Then the cop's walkie talkie went off.

A voice said, "Please go to your car radio immediately."

"I need to go now. Stay safe," the cop said as he headed out the door. My parents looked angry, sad, and frustrated, all at the same time.

My mother stood up and said she was going to run me a bath. That sounded good to me. It meant they wanted privacy. It took a while to get the bath water to the correct temperature. I asked my mother for bubbles, too. That would also give them privacy to talk about whatever they didn't want me to hear. I went into the bath once it was ready, and heard my parents screaming about how they would be able to find heroin. I really liked it better when they weren't high, so I hoped they wouldn't find a new connection. I hoped I would be their main concern. But, I knew it didn't work that way when your parents were junkies. When I didn't want to hear them anymore, I held my nose, went under water and counted how long I could stay under. I made it to eighty-six seconds.

I got out of the bath a little earlier than usual. I felt a bit anxious to watch the news, to see and hear what the media was saying. I asked my dad if he could make Jiffy popcorn and he said yes. *Yay!* After I was out of the bath and in my pajamas, I started making a house with a deck of cards. It was 8:30 p.m. and the news didn't come on until 10:00 p.m. The news always started with one of the anchors saying "It's 10:00 p.m., Do you know where your children are?" I thought that was a stupid question to ask. What if a kid was missing or had passed away? It was a very inconsiderate question. I asked my parents if I could stay up late to watch the news with them. They agreed and said they would record too, in case I fell asleep before it came on. My mother and dad reminded me to not talk to anyone about it, other than them. They said, no matter how annoying or how many questions someone asked. Not one peep, just say "no comment". Even though the cops said it was okay for me to talk to my guidance counselor at school, they said they didn't want me to talk to her either. If the story did go viral, my parents said they wanted to tell the story on one of those talk shows, to whoever offered them the most money. They said the longer we waited, the more the media would pay due to the suspense, just like the cop said. All my parents cared about was their drug money. *Here we go again. My pain, their gain.*

The phone rang and my mother answered it. It was Sam's mother. I heard her say he was allergic to bees. I could only hear one side of the conversation. When my mother hung up, she said Sam's father had a weak heart rate and loss of consciousness. There was also swelling of his face, throat, tongue and lips. She confirmed he was handcuffed to the bed. Sam's mom had told my mother she was planning to divorce him, since he wouldn't even write down his side of the story for her, and that he was going to need both a criminal and divorce lawyer, and she wanted zero to do with his criminal issues. She also apologized on his behalf, and asked my mother how I was doing. She had been able to get away from the members of the media, who had been following her everywhere. She said the FBI had temporary frozen her bank accounts, but she had some money under a mattress which they amazingly hadn't taken, when FBI agents had shown up to search their house. She said she and Sam were staying at a hotel for the time being. My mother hung up, saying the call ended when an operator's voice had cut in and said, "Please deposit ten cents for the next five minutes". Sam's mother said she had to go because she didn't have any more change, but said she would call again soon. I believed her and thought she was a strong woman. She was the type of woman who believed everyone was guilty until proven innocent. Having patience was a very difficult thing to have for so many people since this incident.

The popcorn was ready, and we were all waiting for the news to come on. My sister and brother came home then, at the same time. "What the hell are all these reporters doing here?" My sister asked. I answered, "You'll find out when we watch the news." The news was about thirty minutes away. But, the commercial that was on right then suddenly cut off, and a voice said: "Breaking news. A man is in the hospital tonight, handcuffed to his hospital bed, after allegedly sexually abusing over *twenty* children. Tune in to Fox 5 News at 10:00 p.m., coming up soon, as we are following this developing story. Now, back to your regularly scheduled program. We changed the channel and a rerun of *Three's Company* was on, but it was interrupted only a moment later with the "Breaking News" banner and music. A lady reporter said, "Reporting live from Union City, New Jersey." She was walking backward with the camera following her. "Behind this mausoleum," she said as she motioned toward it, "There is an underground fort where over twenty children, between the ages of five and seven, were allegedly sexually assaulted by a man named Joseph Gonzalez. We have learned that he allegedly lured the children there, by asking them if they wanted a kitten. After each and every sexual assault he allegedly committed against each of these young children, we have been told by multiple sources, that he forced every child to allow him to tattoo a picture of a kitten, along with the word "Whiskers" above the kitten, onto their behinds. Only one child came forward to tell their story, a five-year-old little girl, stating that after the alleged sexual assault and after the accused completed the tattoo on her, a swarm of bees suddenly entered the underground fort and attacked her alleged rapist, allowing her just enough time to escape. Joseph Gonzalez, now in stable condition, is being guarded by members of our local police force. He will be transferred to jail once he is released from the hospital. We have learned he is married and has one child, a young daughter. The whereabouts of his wife and child are currently unknown. We will update you on this story, as it is still developing. Reporting live from Union City. Now, back to regularly-scheduled programming."

Wow. Okay. I had heard enough for one day. I said goodnight to everyone. My mother asked me if I wanted her to tuck me in. "Nah, I'm good," I said. "I'll see you in the morning." I had a hard time going to sleep, tossing and turning. But, I eventually fell asleep by counting sheep again. I thought it was because the bullet-proof vest had been so uncomfortable. When I woke up the next morning, I decided I couldn't handle school that day, so my mother said I could stay home. My dad was supposed to be at work, but for some reason, he came home at 9:30 a.m., sneaking through the back door to avoid the media. When he saw me, he said in a loud, mean voice for me to go straight to my room for missing school. "Do not come out until you are told!" he said, as I ran toward my room. He sounded angry, so I didn't defend myself. I just slammed my door, because I needed love, not to be disciplined. I hadn't done anything wrong! All I could think of was, they must have found a new drug dealer and needed to be high with all the stress and tension with me, plus the media everywhere.

About twenty minutes later, my door slowly opened, and a puppy walked into my room! It was black and white. It was the cutest puppy I had ever seen! I knew right away I was going to call it "Oreo". I checked to see if it was a boy or girl. It was a girl, and I was so happy! I carried her into the living room, as she licked my face. I put her down and hugged my dad. "Thank you, Daddy!" I said. That was the first time I had ever called him "Daddy".

I saw his face as he said, "Wow, you called me 'Daddy', finally! I hope you keep doing that."

I said, "I will, sometimes," and giggled as Oreo kept kissing me. "Mother, look how cute! Her name is Oreo."

My mother said, "That's a great name! You do know a puppy requires a lot of work, right?"

"No worries," I said. "I will feed her, walk her, give her water. But, I will need help with her vet bills. I will take great care of her. I love her!" I knew this puppy would get my mind off everything; even all the bad stuff. I finally had a companion. My father said he would hire a dog trainer within a few weeks, and he showed me where the puppy food was. He laid down puppy pads for Oreo to do her business on. I was so excited. I didn't even want to watch my favorite TV show. All I wanted to do was play with my new baby, Oreo.

With her, I was finally able to laugh and smile. I stared at her as she slept, which she tended to do a lot. I sometimes woke her up to play, but she would go back to sleep. I would sleep too. Sometimes, she would wake me up. It worked both ways, No one liked to have their sleep interrupted. But, if it was for a good purpose, it was worth it. Like, sometimes people needed a cup of coffee and their teeth brushed before they could start their day. Having a puppy was very similar to having a human infant. Oreo needed me to take care of her, and I needed her to take care of me, too. She always did her part. She loved me unconditionally. I wished humans were as loyal as dogs. I mean, if you could find the right companion, great. I hated to compare, but when someone has a dog, they don't have to work on the love because it's automatically there. Some say, that's because dogs don't talk back. But, that's fake news. They do talk back. Only real pet moms and dads know that's true.

I quickly learned Oreo's signs. When she was hungry, she would look at me, then at her food dish, then back at me again. She was so smart and easy to train. When she needed to go out, she would lick my face a bit too much until I would say, "Alright, let's go out." We would sneak through the back door to avoid the people with cameras, the people who wouldn't go away for nothing. When she wanted love, she would snuggle next to me. She didn't care if I was good or bad. She loved me no matter what. She sensed when I was sad, and then cheered me up. She'd scratch her back on the carpet like she was dancing. I took a bunch of pictures of her. In some, she was yawning. I got one with her rolling on her back, with her tongue out. If I cried, which I often did, she would lick the side of my face, and pant with a smile. When I was sick, she would lie on my feet. She was so smart. I loved my Beagle so much.

A dog is a gal's best friend, not just a man's. That's a fact. "Man's best friend…" I bet a man had come up with that expression. I was so happy Oreo was in my life. We helped each other, and I would have given my life for her. I hoped we would die at the same time, because I knew immediately that if one of us outlived the other, we would both be lost. Yes, love could happen that quickly. I was finally experiencing unconditional love. I knew it would be a lot of work to maintain the relationship, but I would do my best. I promised myself I would be the best dog mom, ever!

The next morning, I woke up to puppy kisses; so cute. I walked out to the kitchen. No hot breakfast, but Cheerios would work. At the breakfast table, I asked what "media" was. My mother said, "It's like nosey people trying to get a story first, like what happened to you is a story, a bad story, but still a story. That's how they make their money." I thought that could be my future career, because of my persistence. She then said, "It's all about their moment to be the first to tell this story. Just ignore them, and keep on walking. Don't even look at them. There's more to this than meets the eye." I was like, *Whatever, it's over. What's done is done. I got hurt. He got hurt.* My *God/Karma got revenge. Let's move on.* I was trying to forget, but the media was more persistent then I was. I tried to wake up each morning and not look back. I enjoyed having the attention span of a two-year-old. After all, I had been two years old only three years before. Deep down, I felt like it would never end. It wasn't just about me. I wished the world would revolve around me, just so I could make bad things better.

For whatever reason, no matter how hard you try, somehow, things sometimes won't go your way even if you give it your all. It's hard to let go, when you want to hold on tight to something not meant to be. Like my parents, for example. I wanted to hold on tight to them and wanted to look up to them. But, I couldn't, because they loved drugs more than me. I know I was young, but I didn't understand why some adults were so miserable. I knew there was always at least one person out there, who would say something negative about something positive and innocent. It's as if some people live to insult others, and all you can really do is take care of your closest family and friends. Some people simply love to debate and argue over nonsense. I've learned to never discuss politics, because no good comes from it. When it comes to that topic, it's rare anyone sees eye to eye.

I always love to help strangers in need. The Bible says we should help one another. I have such a strong desire to help, or at least make one person smile every day. I just want to do my best to show someone there is hope, even if it they think their whole world is falling apart. If it looks like they have nothing, something inside of me wants to show them they have something. I want to show them nature, something money can't buy; like a rainbow, or a garden, or skip stones with them on a lake. Or, do something cheap like buy some bread and feed the ducks with them, at Coopers Pond. I feel like I was born to try to do everything in my power to make people's lives simple, instead of complicated. I hate unnecessary complications. My life is complicated, but I am still happy.

I wouldn't allow the Evil Bearded Bee Man to take away my joy. He may have taken it temporarily, but I knew one day I would love life again. That was for sure! I learned something new that day. I learned what media meant. It meant complicated people who wouldn't go away until they got answers; kind of like me. I wasn't allowed to give them any. I turned on the TV and saw a person behind a microphone, live and right outside of my house! I opened the curtains, and looked at the TV. I waved and saw myself on the TV, live like a superstar! *Wow, wow, wow!* I closed the curtains. I hated to swear, but what the hell? I turned the volume up, and the reporter was saying they had gotten a glimpse of the first child who had reported the "Underground Rape Case". *They even came up with a name for it.* I watched myself wave and then close the curtains, on the TV. They played it over and over. My face was on every newscast, and every twenty-four-hour news channel. The story was huge. I hadn't even seen what the newspapers were reporting about it yet, and I wasn't sure if I wanted to know. I knew my life wouldn't be simple for a long time. I felt trapped in my own home because of them. I couldn't go to the park and play with my friends, because they would find me there. It was too close to my house to not be spotted, since I had made the mistake of waving to the media. I was a big star.

4 THE TWISTED TRICK

Once I was ready to go back to school, I was escorted by a police officer who came to pick me up. I needed to get out of the house, and the officer did not allow the media to get near me. I got to sit in the front seat with him. The police officer asked if I wanted to ride with the siren on. I said, "Yes, please! That sounds like fun!" So, he turned on the siren. We got to go through red lights, which I found quite exciting! As we pulled up to the school, the police officer handed me a sealed envelope. He said to put it in my backpack, and not to open it, but to give it to my parents to read. I agreed. I noticed there were about twenty other police cars in the school parking lot, and asked the officer why there were so many.

"We are all going to talk to students in the auditorium about stranger danger," he said. "We're going to have a question and answer assembly for about forty-five minutes this morning." Once inside, I noticed everyone was in school that day, even Sam. She didn't say anything to me. I gave her the evil eye as a warning to not even think about messing with me. We spoke without speaking. As I looked around the classroom, I noticed the girls who didn't raise their hands to make Sam's dad a card, they were the only other ones who had the same type of envelope as the one the cop had given me. I wanted to open it so badly, but I didn't.

When it was time for recess, I got out of my seat and Sam went out of her way to trip me when I was in the hallway. The kids laughed at me. I got up as she walked away, jumped on her back, and knocked her books out of her arms. We both fell. "Come on!" I said loudly. "Get up! Let's end this now!" But, she picked up her books and ran away.

"Way to go, Laura," everyone said to me, cheering me on. I told them to shut up, and two wrongs don't make a right. They were all like, whatever, and walked away. I went to the auditorium to see what the police officers had to say. It was interesting. They had audience participation and taught us all some self-defense moves. They also told us to always wear whistles around our necks, at all times. They explained they were there to serve and protect us, but sometimes the bad guys get away. They said they try their best to keep everyone safe from danger, but sometimes even cops need help.

"If you ever see anything out of the ordinary," one of them said, "please tell a teacher, a parent, a police officer or a firefighter. Tell any trusted adult. Even if it's something weird that just doesn't look right, and you're unsure about it, report it. We are not trying to scare you, but there are a lot of bad people out there. Please do not walk the streets alone, either. *Always* walk with at least one other person, more if possible. And, always cross at crosswalks, at stoplights. No jaywalking. We know you were all told this already, but please be more aware of your surroundings. Well that's a wrap, unless there are any questions?" No one raised their hand, so after telling us to be safe and to be good kids, all of us clapped and then started walking back to our classrooms.

The day went quickly. I kind of wanted to talk to Sam, but I wasn't allowed to. Actions spoke louder than words, but I wanted to know if she was also a victim as well. I kind of felt bad for her. I knew she always bullied me, but I didn't know what had happened to her behind closed doors. I wanted to reach out to her. I heard in a movie once, to keep your friends close but keep your enemies closer. *Maybe I'll apologize tomorrow, even though she started it. I'll sleep on it,* I thought. I only had one more class, gym. My favorite. We were playing basketball that day. It was actually the tie-breaker game. Sam was on the red team and I was on the yellow team. *Why do I see the same color as bees everywhere lately?* I had been practicing basketball at home, and was pretty good at the game. Sam, however, kept charging into me and getting fouled. I would always get the foul ball in. I took one for the team. I took basketball seriously and professionally. She fouled me again, and that time she was out of line.

She tackled me as I went to take a shot, as if we were playing football. I rolled around on the court with her, and punched her in the face. Her nose was bleeding, but I needed her to get off me. She was crazy! The coach sent us both to the principal's office and we were each given detention for a week. Whatever, I didn't care. I just wanted to go home and see what was inside the sealed envelope the cop had given me. When my parents got home after work and had settled in a bit, I told them we all needed to read the letter together. It read,

To Whom It May Concern,

This Saturday, August 22nd, please attended a mandatory meeting from 3:30 p.m. until 7:00 pm at the ice-skating rink on Broadway. This meeting is about the 'Underground Fort Rape Case'. Please keep this meeting confidential.

After the meeting, your child will do a little skating in sync with other victims. Afterward, there will be pizza, soda and snacks. It is mandatory for everyone who lives in your household to attend. We apologize for the short notice. If you have any questions, please contact the Union City Sheriff's office. Thank you.

Best Regards,

UCPD, Union City, New Jersey

After we read it, I was excited and curious. I loved the idea of trying dance ice skating, even though I was much better at roller skating and would probably fall on my butt. I fell a lot, but always got back up. The show must go on. I hoped the other girls were as excited as I was. There had been so much drama, I needed something fun to focus on. *Practice, practice, must practice!* I thought. I knew practice didn't make perfect, but it did make progress. I felt like I was snapping out of my depression and anxiety.

After school that Thursday, I practiced a little bit. I fell of course, but I still had fun doing it. I liked to laugh at my own mistakes. I was a bit sore, so I decided to just watch ice skating on the TV. I hoped since my mother and Daddy had to come, they would enjoy watching me skate. My brother and sister weren't thrilled about going, though. They would have much rather hung out with their friends, than watch some kindergartners ice skating, and

I couldn't blame them. When the day finally came and we arrived at the ice-skating rink, we were all invited to have a seat in the auditorium.

"This event today is not about what the letter said," a police officer announced, once everyone was seated. He looked serious. "There will be no show. You are all here today, because your lives are in grave danger. We have a plan to save you all, but we would like to speak to the parents about it first. We will then explain it to everyone, together. All the children involved in this, I need you to go get into your costumes and put your skates on. Then, sit in a circle and talk to each other until we come back. All siblings, please go to the cafeteria for now. There is plenty of food and some arcade games."

There were twenty-five girls. When we changed into our costumes, we noticed every single one of us had a tattoo of a kitten, with the name "Whiskers". Children talk to other children better than they talk to adults. There were deep breaths and sighs from all of us. I felt sad we had all been raped. To break the ice, I took control and had everyone introduce themselves.

"We all have something in common," I said in a soft voice. "Would anyone like to talk about it or should we just practice?" Everyone agreed we should do both. "Please wait your turn," I continued. "No interruptions. We will sit in a circle and take turns talking. Please do not interrupt each other, and wait your turn to speak." Everyone sat down and made a circle. "Hi, I will start," I said. "I am Laura May. I'm five years old. He lured me into the woods after asking me if I wanted a kitten. I tried to escape, but he pulled my hair and threw me. He tried anal sex, but it kept getting soft. He made me lick and suck him a lot. He took my virginity and he kept my underwear as a souvenir. Bees came into the fort and attacked him. That's when I got away. I am grateful my words made others come forward. That's all." Another girl started to speak.

"Hi, I'm Lisa. I'm six-and-a-half years old. I was riding my bike down a trail one day. I heard a TV and some laughing from an underground fort. I was curious, so I walked down and said hello. There were two guys watching TV. I said, "I'm sorry for trespassing, I was just curious. I have never seen an underground fort with TV before. Impressive!" One of them said, "You know what's impressive? Your ass. Bend over bitch." I made a run for the stairs, but he pulled me back by my hair. Both men took turns raping me. They both laughed as I cried. He put it in an exit, not an entrance. His friend laughed, as he watched. Then his friend did the same thing to me. I cried the whole time. Then he gave me the Whiskers kitten tattoo and he kept my underwear. I believe I am the only kid who had this done by two different men. He knew my name and the names of my family members, and he said they'd die if I tell. They told me to leave, so I left as I was crying."

"Hi, my name is Emma and I'm six years old. All these stories are similar. This monster took our virginity away and our worth! Him giving us souvenirs on our asses is disgusting! Keeping our underwear? Who does that? I am glad he got caught, but he told me he's in a mob. He can get anyone to hurt us or our families, even if he's in jail. I am still scared for my life and families. We all should be."

"Hi, I'm Jamie and I am almost five years old. I shouldn't have followed that man for a kitten. He hurt me and made me cry. Why did that man have to touch me? I just wanted to pet a kitten. He hit me when I tried to escape. I wouldn't have told. But, I decided to tell since Laura did."

"Hi, my name is Katie. I was four-and-a-half years old. I couldn't find my mommy one day at the park. This man said he knew where she was. He carried me into the woods. I don't know why he did things to me. I asked my mom what he was trying to do and she said it was called sex. He put a tattoo of a kitten named Whiskers on my butt, as a present."

"Hi, my name is Alexus. I was four-and-a-half years old. A man with a beard came into my bedroom window. He put sticky tape over my mouth. He brought me to his home in the woods. He put something in my private. I cried, it hurt so much. He drew a kitten named Whiskers, on my butt with a tool. He said to keep it a secret or very bad things would happen to my family. I kicked him and ran away really fast, He couldn't catch me."

"Hi, my name is Victoria. I am five years old. It makes me cry to talk about it. I had sex and got a tattoo of a kitten also. It hurt so much. He scared me and made me shake, inside and out."

"Hi, my name is Janet. I am seven years old. I was in the bathroom at the zoo. A man came into the stall and took me. He said if I yelled, he'd throw me in a lion's cage. He brought me to an underground fort in the woods and he raped me. Then, after, he gave me the kitten tattoo also. His friend was there too. He laughed as he watched."

"Hi, my name is Gloria and I'm six years old. A man who didn't know me was inside of me. I thought I did something wrong. Thanks to Laura, I spoke up. I will never go out alone again."

"Hi, my name is Cheryl. I am five years old. I have nightmares every night now. I wish I didn't go out that day to play. I was right in front of my house when he took me to his underground fort. I will never be the same."

"Hi, my name is Jackie. I am five-and-a-half years old. On my half birthday, a man took away many things from me. Thanks to Laura, he no longer took away my voice. I am no longer allowed to go in my backyard alone anymore."

"Hi, my name is Nicole. I am six years old. I pretended for a long time, that what happened wasn't real. Now that I know others have been through this too, it makes me sad. I hope this never happens to anyone else ever again."

"Hi, my name is Jennifer. I am six years old. This man took away my gentleness. I feel like I am a mean child since this happened. I hope this man understands the damage he has done. I will never be the same because of him."

"Hi, my name is Cathy. I am five years old. The day before this happened, I was proud I no longer needed to sleep with a nightlight on. Now I refuse to sleep without one. I sometimes run into my parents' bed, if I hear any type of noise in the middle of the night."

"Hi, my name is Chelsey. I am seven years old. Every time I see that man's face on the TV, I cringe. I just want to forget about it. I am constantly reminded, and I don't giggle anymore."

"Hi, my name is Betty. I am five years old. I feel like my life is a jigsaw puzzle with pieces all over the place. I hope someday the missing pieces are found. I need to be put back together."

"Hi, my name is Lucy. I just turned five. Every time I see a man with a beard, I get scared. My daddy shaved his off for me. I cry a lot."

"Hi, my name is Emily. I am seven years old. My doctor gave me medicine for panic attacks. I hope they go away someday. I get scared of my own shadow since this happened. I always wake up sweating in the middle of the night."

"Hi, my name is Lynn. I was four-and-a-half years old. I still blame myself for this, because it wouldn't have happened if I hadn't run away from home, because my mom wouldn't let me have chocolate. Everybody said it's not my fault. I still blame myself, and I hate chocolate now."

"Hi, my name is Amanda. I was seven years old. I learned the hard way, what the word 'sex' means. I think I may be a lesbian when I grow up. I think all men except my daddy are mean."

Once everyone was done speaking, I stood up and said, "Now that we got some things off our chests, let's go on the skating rink. We don't know why we are all here today, but let's try to have fun skating until we find out what's going on." Everybody agreed, and we all went on the ice-skating rink and skated.

The costumes were a bit odd looking, and had been hard to put on, but they were sparkly. You could tell they were bulletproof. The parents and cops came back and watched us skate and have fun for a while. I must have fallen on my butt twelve times in ten minutes. I didn't have very good balance. About twenty minutes later, a voice boomed from a loud speaker, and asked us to come off the skating rink for a meeting. Once we were all seated for the meeting, a few plainclothes police officers gathered in front of us. One of them began to speak.

"Children, although this is a grown-up meeting, you all have a right to know what is going on. So, we have invited you all here because each and every one of your lives is going to change. It's not going to be a fun day. Please don't talk until we are done speaking. Also, try to focus and pay attention in this meeting. I need all adults to be silent as well. Children, you will hear many scary things, but try to be strong and understand we need to do certain messed up things, to keep you and your family protected and safe from the friends and associates of the Evil Bearded Bee Man. You have all been through the worst, so we believe you can handle major changes that will happen soon. All of America feels sad for you all, and so many people are lighting candles on your behalf. Not just in the United States, but in pretty much all countries. Although he is in the hospital and will soon be in jail, he still has the power to get his friends to hurt you again, for tattling on him. Sadly, there are TVs in the hospital. He has watched the media coverage of all of this, so he knows you have all spoken up. Even if there wasn't a TV, he would find out, because he has over a hundred evil friends who do bad things. When that many people work together committing crimes, it is called a 'mob' or a 'gang'. You all did the right thing by speaking up, but we need you all to listen *very carefully* now. No talking, please. None of you are going to like what will be happening today. Parents, I need you all to listen very carefully, too. When we are done speaking, we will answer any questions you have. Okay?" Everyone nodded in agreement, and the cop continued.

"Okay. Good. So… We are dealing with one of the most dangerous mobs in America. Since you girls found, or were lured to their hideout, the underground fort, they have emptied it out and have relocated. But, not before we searched it. We found pictures of you girls, numerous pairs of girls' underwear, and a lot of DNA, to keep this man in prison for the rest of his life. We know they warned all of you girls to not tell anyone, or they would kill you and your families. That wasn't said just to frighten you all. This man means business, dangerous business. The mob leader, who all of you know as the Evil Bearded Bee Man, does what he threatens to do; no exceptions. There are so many people in this mob. They believe they are untouchable and can get away with anything. They have been careless lately, since they have gotten away with so much. Now, they are making many mistakes. They are organized, dangerous, demanding, and sneaky. I know you girls were sexually assaulted, all twenty-five of you. We thank all of you for coming here today. We know each of you has been through a horrific experience, and we are trying to catch these bad guys. The members of this mob aren't as smart as they think they are. There are twenty-five girls here today who were victimized by this mob. But, we found thirty-five pairs of girls' underwear in the underground fort. That means, we either have ten girls who haven't come forward possibly due to fear, or ten other girls are among some of many kids who are missing right now. There were pictures found at the scene, but no new faces other than all of yours, so we are not sure at this time. It's under investigation." He motioned to the other two plainclothes officers beside him.

"Joining us today at this meeting are two undercover detectives. Detective Murphy and Detective Smith have both infiltrated this mob. It has taken years of them pretending they are each 'one of them'. Murphy and Smith are originally from the United Kingdom. They moved here to find the American dream and they did find it. They love what they do. They love to protect people. They have changed their accents and appearances. They have the right 'mob' clothes, make-up, masks and wigs… And, they wear bow ties and regular ties. Sometimes, we don't even recognize them. They are very good at their jobs. They both are at the age where they are ready to retire, so that's how we can all help each other. They need to be beyond careful, to not let any members of this mob know they are law enforcement. If they were ever to be found out, the members of this mob would kill them immediately. So, please do not tell *anyone at all* about the two of them pretending to be bad guys. Okay?" Everyone agreed and the cop continued.

"I will say it again. Do not tell *anyone* at all, not even people you think you can trust to keep a secret. It breaks my heart to say this. We know there are hits out for all of you. He wants all of you dead. Somehow, he even knows about Laura's new puppy, Oreo, and he wants her dead, too. He is a very scary monster. The Evil Bearded Bee Man, who is still in the hospital and handcuffed to his bed, wrote to Detective Murphy and Smith, and commanded them to kill all of you girls, who he called 'snitches', plus all of your parents, siblings, and pets. He wrote to them, to not just kill, but to *torture* everyone. He also demanded your pets die slow, painful deaths. We don't know how or who reports everything to him, but he seems to know everything. He also ordered each of your homes robbed, with as much as possible taken." He looked at everyone carefully before continuing. "We know what we are doing, so we have arranged a plan. We have already robbed your homes, and your pets are all in a safe place. You will see them later. We are very sorry, but none of you will be able to go home again. When we robbed your homes, as the Evil Bearded Bee Man ordered, we grabbed as much as we could of value. The good news is, he chose our undercover guys, Detective Smith and Detective Murphy, to kill you all. If he had chosen his own people, we may not have been able to save any of you. When someone is given an illegal job to do, they are not given many details; only names, locations, and a time frame. No questions asked. He simply wrote, *Get it done or there will be consequences.* To give you an example of how this mob works, they hurt people for no reason at all. When someone wants to be in the mob, they must do as they are told, as an initiation. If they are told to hit somebody in the head with a hammer, even in public, they take the hammer and they do it. If they do not get arrested, they get promoted within the mob. If they do get arrested, the mob bails them out and gives them two more chances. Three strikes, they're out, and killed by this mob. That's because they don't want anyone outside of their ranks to know how they operate. None of the members of this mob have a conscience. They are trained to, and they live to, kill and rob, plus rape. Sometimes, it's because of a personal vendetta, or for sex or money… Or, they hurt other people just for kicks and giggles. They are very discreet and cover their tracks well. They come up with ways to make it nearly impossible for them to be caught, and are usually three steps ahead of us. They usually think of everything that could possibly go wrong, and guard against those things going wrong. They are expert criminals. But, as I mentioned earlier, they have been careless lately and are leaving traces behind to make it easier for us to catch them.

"For example, the tattoos were a dumb move because we can now more easily prove it was the same person who committed the crime. They are now sometimes caught for minor crimes, like robbing people's wallets to get money to keep their mob going. With money, comes power. The Evil Bearded Bee Man is the leader of the pack, and probably would have gotten away with all his crimes if it wasn't for the bees that attacked him. Those bees are sweet as honey!" Some kids giggled at that.

"The only time they don't think things through thoroughly, is when they are distracted by sex. When the Evil Bearded Bee Man gives Murphy and Smith a job, they aren't allowed to ask too many questions. Due to the bee attack, his face is swollen, and he has bites all over his body. Let's hear it for Laura and the bees!" Everybody stood up and clapped. "We are so beyond lucky he chose our two undercover officers to get this job done. It could have been done one person at a time. This was the first killing job he ever gave Murphy and Smith, that involved killing more than ninety-nine people. Since he couldn't talk, he wrote down his instructions for them. Now, I'll turn this over to Detective Murphy, who has those instructions and will read them to you." The cop motioned to Detective Murphy. Murphy stepped forward, taking a piece of paper from his pocket and unfolding it.

"Hello everyone," he said. "The Evil Bearded Bee Man's instructions said, 'My daughter Sam told me she overheard a kid talking at school, about how there will be a private dress rehearsal for all the girls who I gave the Whiskers tattoos to. My daughter is ahead of her time. She is my eyes and ears, when it comes to what her classmates are saying and doing. Their parents and siblings will be going to watch their show rehearsal from 4:30 p.m. until 7:00 p.m. tomorrow. The actual show will be the following day. Sam said, the girls who need a break from the media are putting on a show.'" Detective Murphy looked up and said, "On this piece of paper, his daughter wrote down the addresses of all of your homes, to be robbed. Then, she wrote, 'Break a leg, Murph and Smith. Make my Daddy happy and kill them all.'"

I admit I was shocked. *Sam wrote that? How awfu--* Detective Murphy's voice interrupted my thoughts. "For a person to get his five-year-old child to do his dirty work is beyond unacceptable." The detective continued. Sam had also written the request that I be killed last, so I would have to watch my friends die first. Wow, the apple didn't fall from the tree! She was pure evil. She had obviously lied to her mom, unless her mom had been putting on some "I am innocent" act, to avoid jail. I liked Sam's mom, but you really couldn't trust anyone. After hearing what Sam had written to Murphy and Smith, I no longer felt bad for her at all.

Detective Murphy turned over the paper. "On this side," he said, "the Evil Bearded Bee Man wrote a note to myself and Detective Smith. 'Murphy and Smith, I want you to go to all these addresses starting at 4:00 p.m. I don't care if they are home or not. I want them all robbed. Take as much jewelry and cash as possible. If you see a dog or cat, kill it. Kill any witnesses. Do not go to the school, until you've robbed every address. I want you to put everything you've stolen behind the dumpster over on Thirty-Sixth Street. There will be a man in black pants and a ski mask. Hand everything over to him and he will give you two loaded machine guns, plus extra ammunition. Then, you are to go to the school and shoot every kid on the stage, and everyone in the audience as well. Then, you both get out of there as soon as you can. We are counting on you to kill close to one hundred people. It's your first major assignment. We trust you and it pays great. I want everything you do video recorded as well. You got this! When you're done, bring the video to my daughter, Sam, who will be waiting at the dumpster. Then, go home, enjoy, make popcorn and watch the news."

Detective Murphy looked up from the paper. "That's it." He folded the paper and put it into his pocket. "After Detective Smith and I read this, we said 'consider it done' to Joseph Gonzalez, the man you girls know as the Evil Bearded Bee Man. He nodded at us and winked. When this man nods and winks, that means he is happy. We thanked him for the opportunity, told him to feel better and that we wouldn't let him down. He respects and trusts both of us. Plus, he has allowed two of our other detectives to join his mob without initiation, since Smith and I both highly recommended them. They will be taking our places, since we are both retiring. We had a very long run with this mob. We have even been able to provide the dead bodies of people who died naturally, because after all, we are the police. They may be a few steps ahead, but we have tricked them on several occasions. There are many people who they believed died, who are living well in a witness relocation center. We had the newspaper print fake obituaries. Since we are both retiring after this final job, we are going to have to fake our own deaths. To keep you all safe, everyone in this room will be faking their own deaths as well. We have carefully thought out a plan that will work, thanks to the police, paramedics, CIA and last but not least, the FBI. While you girls are pretending to be doing a fundraising show, Detective Smith and I are going to shoot all of you girls on the ice-skating rink, with a machine gun filled with blank rounds. You girls will all have bulletproof bodysuits on, underneath your costumes. The blank bullets will have red paintball markers in them. It will be just like when you play paintball. We will be close to the stage when we shoot you girls. We will then turn around and shoot all the parents and siblings who are sitting in the audience. The adults, of course, will all be given bulletproof vests as well. When you get shot by blank rounds, it will hurt a little. But, you all must try your *very* best to not react. Can you do that?" All the kids agreed, and

Detective Murphy continued.

"The ambulances will arrive and put everyone in body bags. They will have holes so you can each breathe just fine, so don't worry. The police will be there as well. They will all know it's fake, too. After this fictitious bloody massacre, a bunch of police officers will shoot blank rounds at both myself and Detective Smith. This letter, with instructions from the Evil Bearded Bee Man will be found in my pocket and will be read to the media. Like we said, this guy is getting careless which will lead to him getting caught. It's going to be loud, so wear earplugs. There is a bag of earplugs stage right. The two of us will also be leaving in body bags. Every police officer on the scene will know we are all pretending to be dead. We need this to look totally real, with *zero* mistakes. I know this isn't fun stuff and I apologize for that. But, we will make it up to all of you. That's a promise. All the paramedics will know this isn't real, but they will act as if it is. The members of the media, however, will believe it's real, and none of them will be allowed inside the hospital. One or more members of our law enforcement will go live on TV and explain that this is a horrific tragedy where two police officers, twenty-five children who were performing on stage, twenty-two of their siblings and fifty parents, were all shot and killed. They will also tell the media that the two gunmen were shot and killed, as well, leaving a total of ninety-nine people dead. No survivors. The media will also be told: 'Even though it's not yet confirmed, we believe all the children performing on stage were all victims of the Underground Fort rape case, and we have reason to believe this was a mob-related crime.' Also, the president of the United States, President Jimmy Carter, knows this event will be fake. But, he will be making a speech to make it look real. This 'mass murder' is going to be all over the news for several days, and will go worldwide. No one can make any mistakes. This must be flawless and beyond convincing. You all need to be very good actors and actresses, because the lives and careers of many people depend upon it. The members of the media will certainly be working a lot of overtime." Detective Murphy paused and looked at everyone carefully. "Is everyone with me so far?" The kids and parents nodded and mumbled in agreement.

"Okay, good." Detective Murphy continued. "As all of us are put into body bags and loaded into ambulances, we must stay completely still. Do not scratch or move, *at all.* Just try your best to not make any movement at all.

Two seconds after you hear a loud bang, take a deep breath, drop to the floor and remain completely still, while holding your breath for as long as you can. Remember, all of this is going to be video recorded and it must appear real. Count, 'one Mississippi, two Mississippi,' and then drop to the floor. As each ambulance arrives at the hospital, the paramedics will bring you up to the roof and into a helicopter. My children and Detective Smith's children, along with Oreo and everyone else's pets and personal belongings, will be waiting for us at our destination. I know this is a lot to take in, especially at your age. But, everything will be okay. Trust us. We know what we are doing. And, I must repeat myself: *please* remember, under *no* circumstances are you to speak one word of any of this, to anyone, not *ever*. Understood?" We all agreed. Detective Murphy continued.

"You and many others will die if you do. The members of this mob are heartless. I know people like to talk, but when it comes to this, every single one of you must 'zip it, lock it, and put it in your pocket.' Thankfully, the media won't be allowed inside the hospital. Now, back to exactly what will happen… Once you are loaded into a helicopter, still pretending to be dead inside of your body bag of course, someone will then unzip the bag onboard the helicopter, and you will be on your way out of the country. The helicopters will be news reporter choppers, so people will believe all the helicopters are just trying to get photos and video coverage. We already have passports for all of you. You will each be given a new name, identity and address. You will be given your passports once we arrive at your new home. That's when you will know your new names. Once again, I know this is life changing. It's going to be difficult to leave your extended family and friends behind, without even saying goodbye. You have all been through a lot, and I understand moving brings even more stress. But, in time, you will all adjust to your new lives. It is amazing what time and a fresh start can do. Sometimes, a big change can be really cool. Life is what you make of it, and I believe all your futures will be amazing." Detective Murphy smiled before continuing. I guess he was trying to make us all feel like this was an adventure.

"I feel the need to repeat myself," he said, his smile fading into a serious look. "I want to make sure this one thing is seared into your brains. Do not tell *anyone* about this. *No one. Not ever.* Not even ten or twenty years from now. You all must pretend *none* of this ever happened. As I said before, people's lives depend on it. If you do, it will just be a matter of time until they spot *all of you,* and then none of you will ever be safe. It's possible you could all be murdered, the second they track you all down. These bad people are all over the place. We are going overseas to a very safe place, but still, none of you can tell anyone where you are living, not even your close relatives. Everyone must believe you were murdered. If you do slip up and say anything, and any members of this mob find out somehow, they will find you and torture you and kill you, every single one of you. I know most of you are in kindergarten, so parents, please talk to your children about this. Threaten consequences if you have to, if they say anything. I know some of you have dollar signs in your eyes and want to negotiate with news channels or talk shows, if the price is right. Once we move, I promise you all this: we have a lot more to offer you financially, than any talk show, or magazine, whatever. We will draw up contracts that will be more than generous. This mob will probably be cheering that all of you were shot and killed, but they will be upset about losing myself and Smith. The Evil Bearded Bee Man will be upset no video was delivered to him, but a video will make it into the media's hands after our editing is done. They will all have their headlines and their work cut out for them. But, you all will probably be swimming in a pool and doing the doggie paddle with Oreo, if this goes as flawlessly as we expect."

Emma shouted out, "Wait, we are going to have a swimming pool?"

Detective Murphy smiled at her, and nodded. "If all goes as planned, we will supply all of you with housing, clothing, food, shelter, swimming pools, and cash. Pretty much everything you need."

"Where are we moving to?" Another child asked.

"We don't want *anyone* to know where we are going. That is why you all won't find out until we get there. We guarantee you will all be safe, and you will be living in a beautiful place. Here's the part you are going to hate. None of your other relatives or friends can ever know you are all still alive. I know that's heartbreaking, especially for the kids. But, at least each of you kids are young enough to start a whole new life. No looking back. We will send you each copies of the video recordings of your memorial services, if you wish, so you can see everyone saying goodbye to you. Every casket will be closed, of course. You will more than likely see footage of your services on the news, as this story will be *huge*. I know this mob well. They are unreasonable and as evil as evil can get. We set it up so everyone will have an obituary as well: ninety-nine fake obituaries. They are already printed up and in a safe place. We have all worked very hard to make sure you will all be safe. So, you each need to do your part and do everything I just told you to do. I'm sorry you all have to leave so suddenly, and I am sorry you will never see your homes again. But, remember… The alternative is dying for real. This is all for your own safety." As I listened, I thought, *it's my home, not just a house.* Murphy continued.

"Do not worry about your futures. You will all be very well taken care of. Money will be no object. We are helping you as much as you are helping us. Detective Smith and I need to do this, fake our own deaths, to get out of this mob, and all of you need to be in a safe location so you can you're your lives without fear of being killed by the members of this mob. It's a win-win situation, except for parting with your loved ones. The two undercover detectives who are replacing myself and Detective Smith, will keep an eye on this mob, so we can take them down one by one. Having their leader in prison will be a good start, but our replacements need to be trusted and respected. Sam likes the replacement guys, and they are communicating well with her. Now, does anyone have any questions?"

Q: What if we refuse to go with you and move somewhere else instead?

A: I highly recommend you *not* do that. We have gone above and beyond to protect you all. If you are spotted, this mob will do a search, and look and find answers. Your pictures are going to be all over the news. It is much safer to move out of the country. Everybody there speaks English.

Q: Are you saying we have to leave today, just like that?

A: Yes. The alternative is living in fear all the time. Also, the high risk of you being murdered. We understand change is scary. You and your children will be safer this way. Also, you will no longer be questioned or followed by the media.

Q: Why wouldn't this pretend fundraising show only be available for the parents and siblings to watch?

A: Good question. We have flyers and advertisements up, stating the actual show is tomorrow. Everyone believes today is a private rehearsal, for immediate family only. We set it up, so Sam could overhear what we wanted her to report to her father. Obviously, there will not be a show for the public tomorrow.

Q: Will we have American TV channels where we are going?

A: Yes, you will have a satellite dish, plus a beautiful home. You all should be excited for this move. It's spectacular. It is much safer than Union City. You will all have swimming pools, hot tubs and balconies. It will all be paid for in full, even the property taxes. Transportation will also be provided, no worries. You'll see when we arrive.

Q: What about getting a job, earning income?

A: That won't be necessary. But, if you want to work, you can. However, your living expenses will be paid for indefinitely.

Q: You said we will have new names. Will we have new social security numbers and birth certificates?

A: Correct. You will all have new names, and yes, new birth certificates and passports. No new social security numbers though, as you will no longer be US citizens. But, we will have all the documentation we each need, where we are all going.

Q: Will the kids all go to public school?

A: No. For safety, all the kids will be homeschooled.

Q: How do we know the media won't offer more than you, if we can't even speak to them about any of this?

A: You will all have offers no one would ever refuse. Just be patient. Let us get you out of the country so you are safe. Then, we will explain everything, and draw up written contracts for each of your families. Remember, *we* are saving your lives. The media is not. They just want a juicy story. We want you and your family protected, alive and healthy. No news channel or talk show can offer you that.

"Are there any other questions?" No one else raised their hand or spoke up. Everyone looked disappointed and anxious at the same time. "Okay everyone, let's do this. Follow me," the detective said.

All the parents and girls followed him into the large ice rink and the girls began skating around. The detective said, "It's almost show time!" He then said, "Okay, quick recap. In a few minutes, you will hear loud bangs. After you hear them, count to three and then drop to the ground. Do not move, get up, scratch, cough, move your head or stretch… nothing. All of you stay still. Keep your eyes open while you are playing dead, and try your best to not blink. We will then turn around and fire several shots at the parents. I need siblings and parents to try and get up to run toward your girls. We will be filming, so make it look real. While you're running toward them, drop to the ground immediately. Most of the shots will be fired near you but not at you, so just drop when you hear them. This place will be dark, except for the spotlights on the girls who are supposedly performing, so the video will not turn out that great, even with editing. There will be over three hundred blank rounds, shot from the machine guns. If one of the blank bullets does hit you, it will hurt a little. But, try to not react. Just drop to the ice. I am sorry for repeating myself, but you all must understand how important it is to stay still on the ground. Pretend you're all actors, auditioning to be in movie. Use your imagination and make it look real. When the paramedics arrive, they will close your eyes with their fingers. Be sure to keep them closed. I am so sorry you all must experience this, but it will be over fast. Okay. In one minute, it's show-time. Everyone put in your earplugs."

The detectives made sure no one was in the building, and locked the doors until it was time for them to open them up. It was very loud, but thankfully, everything went as planned. At least we hoped so. Everyone was playing dead. They could have all won Emmy awards for their performances. The two undercover detectives, Murphy and Smith, ran to the door, pretending to get away. That is when the police shot the two detectives with blank rounds, and they dropped and played dead as well. Then, all the ambulances started arriving. They were professionals and started to put everyone in body bags as quickly as possible. The police and ambulances were everywhere. The Swat team arrived, and the road was closed. The yellow tape was put up. There were barricades, so the media wasn't allowed to get close. It took about an hour to get ninety-nine bodies, in different sized body bags, into all the ambulances. Helicopters took off as soon as 'the bodies' were brought to the roof of the hospital.

Each of us was allowed to move around more freely once our body bag was unzipped, after the doors of each helicopter closed. All the helicopters flew over the scene, just to make it look like it was news. They then headed for their destination. They had to make one stop to refuel, but ended up arriving on time at the destination. Ninety-nine people arrived safely, after a six-hour ride in the sky aboard numerous helicopters.

We all met at a house the size of a mansion. Detective Smith and Detective Murphy invited us in. The ceilings were at least fifty feet high. It was the biggest place I had ever seen. We must have walked thirty minutes just to get to a room that could comfortably seat a hundred people. We all walked in and Oreo came running straight to me. I was so happy to see her. She gave me tons of puppy kisses.

"Where is my dog?" Amanda asked.

Detective Murphy said, "All of you will get to see your pets shortly. Laura got to see her puppy first, because she is the reason you all came forward. You followed her lead, which saved your lives. This question is for the children only. Does anyone know what country we are in? If you do, raise your hand." No one raised their hand. "We are in London, England. You all will be living in this palace. Each of you will either have your own room or will share with your siblings. That is your choice. There are itineraries in everyone's rooms." A parent interrupted.

"How in the world can you afford this for us, on a cop's salary?"

"Okay, I will tell you how," said Detective Murphy. "Before I moved to the United States, I was the Queen's bodyguard. I had saved her life by taking a bullet meant for her, while we were in public once. I was shot in the head and barely survived. If the bullet had entered a fraction of an inch to the left, I would have been dead. While I was in the hospital, The Queen told me if I ever needed anything, to please ask and consider it done. That was a few years ago. Two weeks ago, I sent her an email, asking if she could offer a safe place for almost a hundred people and a few dogs to live, because their lives were in danger from one of the most dangerous mobs in the US. I explained that Detective Smith and I had worked undercover for the mob, and needed to retire. We also needed to save twenty-five families, plus their pets, from the mob. I asked her if she could help. She wrote back immediately, 'Your wish is my command.' Before her daughter's tragic death, she had the Prince help her build a mansion for over one hundred lucky children who had been living in poverty. It is in Buckingham Palace's backyard, several acres away from the Palace. After she received my email, she forwarded it to the Prince. The Prince agreed to have us all live there. He said the Princess, may she rest in peace, would have also agreed if she were still alive, because it would be saving children from danger. He also said he knew I had saved his mother, the Queen's life, so he didn't even need time to think about it. He immediately answered her, saying we could all stay as long as needed, with VIP treatment. He also said, this place is not known to the public. There are guards, even changing of the guards for training purposes. They will protect all of us. Those kids and parents hit the jackpot. However, they must learn how to live like wealthy people live. The Prince said he will invite all of us over for dinner at Buckingham Palace, in a month or so. In the meantime, there is a credit card on the kitchen table. Take them clothes shopping and get them all haircuts. Make sure their hair is dyed so they do not look like themselves since their pictures are all over the news. The parents, too. Hire a tutor to teach them how we talk and walk like a Brit. The Prince said he had researched Union City, New Jersey in the USA, and saw how these kids had been brought up on the wrong side of the tracks. So, he prefers to meet them after they change their appearance. I thanked the Queen. She wrote back that she wouldn't be able to have a conversation with anyone if it wasn't for me saving her life."

Wow, we were all going from rags to riches, I thought. I hoped my parents wouldn't get themselves kicked out of here. If they got kicked out, due to their bad habits and addiction issues, then they were dumber than I thought they were, if that was at all possible. They were getting a second chance at life, so if they tried to find a drug connection, I was sure they would get kicked out. Hopefully, me and my brother and sister would be allowed to stay. Maybe they would make our parents go to a rehab. Time would tell. In the meantime, I felt like Little Orphan Annie when she first arrived at Daddy Warbuck's house. The maid came in. "You are all still on East Coast time," she said, "and there is a six-hour difference here. I would like for you all to pick any bedroom. They are all fully furnished. Meet here at 8:00 a.m. sharp tomorrow, for breakfast and a full tour. Good night all." We all said goodnight in stereo, and scattered to find a room to sleep in. The bed I chose was so comfortable, I fell asleep right away. I didn't even need to count sheep.

The next morning when I woke up, I had forgotten where I was. Then, I looked around at the beautiful room my siblings had refused to share with me. They had wanted their own room and I couldn't blame them. Even though I knew I was in a safer place, I still saw the Evil Bearded Bee Man in my nightmares. Having a room all to myself was a bit scary due to my age and the fact I was used to always sharing a room. I would try to adjust, or maybe even sleep with my parents if they remained clean and sober. I had smelled alcohol on their breath recently, but they weren't doing heroin. At least, I didn't think they were. The social workers thought they were dead, so they had dodged drug testing. Maybe they needed to feel some sort of drug, so they drank more. At least alcohol was legal, and maybe the palace would cause them to want to change their ways for the better, or maybe for the worse. If they didn't need to work and got free money from the Queen, they would probably spend it foolishly. I had been told, once someone reached a certain older age, like fifty, they wouldn't change. I hoped that wasn't true.

I looked up and noticed there was a huge flat screen TV in my room. I had been too tired to notice it the day before. It was as if I was in a movie theater! I turned it on and saw the ice-skating rink was on the TV. I changed the channel and it was on every channel, so I decided to watch before I had to go downstairs. I was surprised it was on every channel in England. But, then again, nearly a hundred people had been "murdered". I had forty-five minutes before I had to be at the breakfast table. The itinerary was clear: 8:00 a.m. sharp, no exceptions. I hated rules, but I needed to change my attitude while I was still young enough to do so. I was one lucky kid to be able to live behind Buckingham Palace. It was as if I was living in a real-life fairy tale. There was a King, a Queen, a Princess and a Prince. I could even meet a real Prince Charming one day. I flipped the channel again, because I didn't want to think about the Evil Bearded Bee Man. But, curiosity got the best of me, so I started to watch. The Detectives were correct. The news lady was in behind the barricade, filming all the dead bodies going into the ambulances.

She said, "Hi, I'm Brook Cassidy. Yesterday afternoon at this ice-skating rink, ninety-nine people were shot dead during a children's show rehearsal, located in Union City, New Jersey. We believe Joseph Gonzalez, known to the girls as the Evil Bearded Bee Man, is allegedly the mastermind behind these shootings. The shooters, Michael Smith and Julio Murphy were both shot and killed by Officer Wilson of the Union City Police Department. It is confirmed all the victims who were murdered, were all the children who were involved in the Underground Fort rape case." They each had a tattoo of a picture of a cat, with the name 'Whiskers' written above it, according to the Union City Police Department. As this story is developing, we believe Joseph Gonzalez, who is the leader of one of the most dangerous mobs in the United States, sent Michael Smith and James Murphy to kill these children, and their siblings and parents. Their homes were also robbed and their pets killed, as the children's parents and siblings were watching the children rehearse for a benefit show that would have taking place today, had it not been for this tragedy. Joseph Gonzalez's wife and only child, a young daughter, were found at a motel by an anonymous tipster, and have been brought in for questioning. They are still under interrogation at the police station. Joseph Gonzalez, who was just released from the hospital today, is in prison without bail. He is in solitary confinement. He wrote to the police, since he still can't yet talk due to an allergic reaction to bee stings, he is glad they are all dead and will not be able to have their day in Court. Those words don't make him look good, but also does not prove he is guilty. The jury won't like that at all. Joseph Gonzalez is pleading 'not guilty' on all counts. The prosecutors claim they have enough evidence from lab results, to put him in prison for life, on raping and kidnapping charges. If he is found guilty of these killings, the death penalty is also a possibility. As their deaths are still under investigation, he cannot be charged with murder just yet. But, the letter with the orders that were giving by Joseph Gonzalez, in his hand writing, won't help his case at all. Words are never misconstrued, when they are in writing. He is not yet charged with their murders, since he was in the hospital at the time of the shootings. The police believe he is guilty, because he sent people to shoot them all. They just need time to prove it. Joseph Gonzalez wrote down that he is pleading the fifth. They police are telling the press that James Murphy, fifty-nine years old, lived in Manhattan with the other shooter Michael Smith, sixty-two years old. The police got a warrant to check their home. It was a very clean and organized two-bedroom apartment. There was a note found in one of the shooters pockets that gave directions to shoot and kill everyone at the rehearsal. The note was allegedly in a child's handwriting along with an adult's handwriting. They believe Josephs Gonzalez's young daughter wrote part of the note. The note also mentioned that his daughter, only five years old, somehow knew this was going to take place but didn't tell anyone. In fact, she wrote on that paper to rob victims' homes and kill their animals. She also wrote down all the victims' addresses, that she somehow got from school. She also wrote to please kill "Laura" last, so she could "watch her friends, family and sibling die." On the other side of the note, was the Evil Bearded Bee Man's handwriting. He wrote instructions to rob all the homes, kill all the pets, and steal as much as possible. He then wrote to bring the stolen merchandise to a dumpster on Thirty-Sixth Street. Hand the stolen items to a man in a ski mask. He will hand you a machine gun. The exchange was made on camera, but the man couldn't be identified. The machine guns were untraceable. According to local police, the man took the stolen items, said "good luck" and took off. It's a mystery how a five-year-old child could take part in something as awful as this. But, maybe we'll learn more soon, considering the child and her mother are being interrogated by law enforcement, right now. We will have more on this story later, and President Carter will be speaking about it as well, later this evening."

Another reporter started talking about something else, and I turned off the TV to get ready for breakfast. I was thinking about how well-planned out everything had been, and how the police were making sure the truth didn't come out. The police officers who were talking live on TV were distracting the public from the shooter's backgrounds as much as possible, so the Evil Bearded Bee Man would be the main concern and not the two "dead" shooters: Detective Murphy and Detective Smith. That was smart. The police are guiding the media and the public toward concentrating more on the Evil Bearded Bee Man, since he is the leader of the mob. They are also trying to make the media and the public focus more on the kindergarteners' memorial services. If the press found out Murphy and Smith were members of law enforcement, it could ruin everything.

The two undercover detectives who took their places within the mob, could continue to report everything to the police, about the mob's upcoming plans, while their leader sat in jail. Murphy and Smith's home had been staged, as if they were a gay couple living together. If Joseph Gonzalez found out about their sexuality, the police didn't believe he would care, since they had always done what they were told. It would keep the media busy, reporting on their sexuality, instead of what they had done for a living. In 1977, being gay was a huge deal. The media would have fun with that part of the story. The police could easily deny them being detectives too, if need be, since Murphy and Smith had always dressed differently anyway.

Plus, we had the FBI and CIA on our side, and they would make sure they were safe. Their two replacements should be safe too, and be able to report everything the mob had planned, coming up. They had been trained by the best, Murphy and Smith, so they were surely trying on all types of different clothing. Most people knew there was a lot of propaganda in the news. But, for some reason, people always believe everything they hear on TV, because it was on the news. Sometimes, news can be fake, but no one seemed to question it in the 1970s.

If the news got out to the media, about Detective Murphy and Smith being detectives in the mob, their two replacements would be picked up and put into witness relocation immediately, for their own safety. Joseph Gonzalez just needed to know from the media, that Smith and Murphy were the killers, and were now dead. We couldn't have the lives of the two detectives who took their places, in danger. According to everything Detective Murphy had said, the goal was to break up this mob somehow.

The cops would make sure the jail would take away his TV privileges, and keep him in solitary confinement. A cop had set him up for stealing by planting a weapon on him. That way, he could be in solitary confinement for the maximum time allowed by law. His trial would start within a few weeks, according to the district attorney's office. The police were saying that even without the girls' testimony in Court, since they are all deceased, he would still most likely be sentenced to life in prison, possibly even death row.

The police had been notified that Joseph Gonzalez had hired the most expensive, respected lawyer in the United States. His lawyer could find the slightest mistakes made by the prosecution and was well-known for setting hardcore criminals free, on the smallest technicality. Sadly, the Evil Bearded Bee Man, also known as Joseph Gonzalez, could afford him due to mob money he had obviously hidden away from the authorities. When the prosecution found out who his lawyer was, they immediately asked for a meeting with the judge who would be handling the case. The judge was in Court, so his clerk told them they could speak to him after Court had adjourned. The prosecutors had never won a case against the Evil Bearded Bee Man's lawyer. The lawyer's rate was almost unheard of, $2,500-per-hour. If this lawyer were to dig deep enough to somehow discover that law enforcement knew all ninety-nine people were alive, the two undercover detectives in Joseph Gonzalez's mob would be killed for being cops, possibly even beheaded, or hung, or held for ransom, or even slowly tortured to death. Law enforcement was being very careful they remain safe at all times. If the media got wind this had all been fake, and no one had really been murdered, there would be total chaos.

Waiting for Court to be over was taking a long time. Detective Wilson was there with the prosecution, waiting. He couldn't wait to explain it to the judge. The judge had the most power in that Courtroom, and Detective Wilson knew Joseph's $2,500-per-hour lawyer was also the judge's son-in-law. The detective was also a close friend of the family, and had even babysit the judge's son-in-law when he was a child. Hopefully, that friendship would compel the judge to overrule certain questions that could be irrelevant. He would have to express his concerns and come clean. If the judge knew that not just local law enforcement, but the CIA and FBI were in on the staged mass murder as well, the judge may be upset that they were trying to make a mockery of the system.

Joseph Gonzalez had raped and abused dozens of children, and had ordered ninety-nine people killed. Hopefully, the president of the United States would personally speak to both the judge and the Evil Bearded Bee Man's lawyer. President Carter would make sure no one would have anything to worry about. The president had not yet returned any phone calls regarding this urgent matter, but the detectives were sure he would help them tie up any loose ends; at least they hoped he would. They requested President Carter also speak with the Evil Bearded Bee Man's lawyer and give him an offer he couldn't refuse, to do his part to ensure Joseph Gonzalez would be found guilty at trial. Knowing President Carter would help them, was a huge weight off many shoulders. He would make this right and had many tricks up his sleeve, to protect the innocents involved. Everything should go as planned, especially since the Queen of England, the FBI and the CIA were all on our side. The lies would set us free. If it wasn't for Detective Smith and Detective Murphy working undercover inside this mob, all these girls would be dead.

Detective Wilson couldn't wait to talk to the judge. He would also mention the Queen was helping the victims and their families in this situation, and hoped that would assist in putting Joseph Gonzalez away for a long time. Bottom line was, everyone needed for this top lawyer to either lose his first case ever, out of thousands, or at least withdraw from the case, saying he no longer wished to represent the defendant, Joseph Gonzalez. In addition, Detective Wilson planned to request from the judge, that the media and public not be permitted inside the courtroom. He hoped the lawyer would have a heart and take one for the team. Detective Wilson was going to try his best to have a private, one-on-one conversation with the judge, to hopefully convince him to convince his son-in-law to back off and drop Joseph Gonzalez as his client. The detective had his fingers crossed as he impatiently waited to speak to the judge. He even took a Valium. This case was giving him high anxiety.

Meanwhile, in England, I had time to watch one more TV newscast, before breakfast time. I was glued to the TV, as I listened to the newscaster speak. "Joseph Gonzalez sustained hundreds of bee stings and is still unable to talk, due his face, lips and tongue being so swollen. He remains on a breathing tube as well, due to that immense swelling. It is also hard for him to urinate, due to several bee stings in his private area. He is allergic to bees, and his entire body was stung over one hundred times before medical personnel were called to the scene, due to an anonymous 9-1-1 call made by a child. We believe that child was the first one to come forward in this, the Underground Fort rape case. Her name was Laura May and after she came forward, twenty-four other children found the courage to come forward as well. But, in this case, no good deed goes unpunished. Laura May died a hero, along with the other twenty-four children, and their parents and siblings. All were shot and killed yesterday, allegedly by order of Joseph Gonzalez, the leader of one of the most dangerous mobs in the entire country. One of the things Joseph Gonzalez wrote down for us, again, because he is unable to speak, was this: 'I am not admitting I had anything to do with their deaths.' He also revealed he was only saddened by the deaths of two of the members of his mob, the two shooters. That statement right there, it doesn't admit guilt, but no member of the jury will like it... If he is put on trial for these horrific crimes." *Wow. This man isn't the brightest crayon in the box*, I thought. Yet, he's the leader of a mob that has gotten away with many crimes. The newscaster's voice continued:

"He will not speak about his daughter, regarding whether or not she was trained by him to think and work with evil people. He will not write down anything about his wife, except for calling her some choice names that I cannot repeat here on the air, because she is divorcing him. He wrote to us, that 'she took a vow for better or worse' and 'her requesting a divorce during the worst, is double-crossing me'. Also, and surprisingly, he also told us in writing, 'She will pay for this.' But, he refused to write down *how* she would pay for it." The newscaster moved on to reporting on the upcoming memorial services.

"There will be a memorial this Friday. With me right now are the aunt and godmother of Emily Levi, one of the many young children shot and killed." Emily's Aunt Cheryl had tears rolling down her face, as she held the reporter's microphone.

"We were planning on having cake for Emily's fifth birthday this Saturday," the aunt said. "Instead, we are planning her funeral. It's devastating. She was a sweet little girl who was always smiling and had so much energy. Two tragedies in one week. I am lost for words." The reporter took the microphone back as she told Emily's aunt how sorry she was for her loss.

"God bless all those little children," the reporter said. "And, may He bless their parents and siblings and pets, in heaven. Most of the victim's relative have refused to speak with us, because they are too upset." The camera then panned over hundreds of items, all part of a makeshift memorial that had popped up overnight. "There are hundreds of teddy bears, flowers, cards, candles and posters here, in front of this ice-skating rink, honoring the victims." The camera went back to the reporter's face. "This story is still developing," she said. "Please tune in to Fox 5 at 6:00 p.m. tonight for the latest developments."

I turned off the TV, so I wouldn't be late on the first day of breakfast in my new *home*, not just a *house*. The itinerary seemed demanding, filled with many activities. I knew we must be on time for breakfast, lunch and dinner, but I wasn't sure if the activities were mandatory. Either way was fine with me, though. I hadn't finished reading the itinerary just yet, but I had noticed horseback riding, tennis lessons and swimming lessons. Oreo was still sleeping soundly in her crate, so I let her be. I left the itinerary on my bed and headed to breakfast. The place was so big, I got a little lost. But, I found the dining room just in time. Wow, the table was long enough to seat a hundred people. There were only three empty chairs, and enough food on the table to feed an army. All ninety-nine of us were there. I was impressed my whole family had made it on time. It was nice to know the eggs wouldn't have eggshells in them. We were all hungry. Airplane food stinks. A few kids were told to sit up straight by the maid, and to put napkins in their laps. I was sure there would be many more rules, but living there was worth it. We all had a gourmet breakfast that had everything I could think of, in addition to food I couldn't even identify. Afterward, we were told to go brush our teeth and take showers, not by our parents, but by the maid who seemed to be in charge. She was a large, black, loudly-spoken woman. We all looked at our parents for approval. They said to always do what we were told to do, by anyone in uniform. I was used to taking baths, so I asked my daddy to teach me how to get the water to become a shower.

The maid interrupted and said, "Baths are also allowed, if you prefer them over showers".

I said, "Thank you, but I would like to see if I will like showers better. I never tried one yet."

He said, "Okay, Buttercup," and lifted me up onto his shoulders. I loved when he did that. With his help, I took my first shower ever, and really liked it. I felt like I had graduated and had more of a spring to my step.

I went back to my room to read the itinerary dated for that day. Tomorrow's would be different. Breakfast ended at 9:00 a.m. it said. Shower time from 9:05 a.m. until 10:00 a.m. At 10:15 a.m. everyone needed to be at the salon, to have their hair done. That was for both children and adults. The itinerary was very detailed. It stated long hair will be cut and all our hair would be dyed to whatever color we each chose. All animals should be brought to the second floor where they will be groomed and trained. If anyone has tattoos, they will be removed. As far as piercings, minor children are only allowed to have pierced ears, one hole in each ear. If any of you have piercings anywhere else, or more than one piercing in each ear, those additional piercings will be sealed closed, no matter where they are located. We have the equipment and professionals to take care of these tattoos and extra piercings with very little pain. The younger children will go first, since their kitten tattoos were given to them against their wills. We only have three tattoo professionals with us today, so please be patient until it's your turn. Everyone will also be getting a full body massage today. As the younger girls are getting their tattoos removed, the older kids are to go to the next room for your full body massages and facials. You will be naked during the massages, and your masseuse will note all your tattoos and piercings, in a private room. You will then get back into your robe and wait for your massage. When the younger girls are done, your tattoo removals will be done.

I was sure, especially the teenagers wouldn't be happy about having their tattoos and piercings removed. But, it was the Queen's orders. We had already been told that no one, and I mean *no one*, questioned the Queen or disapproved of any choice the Queen made. Somebody had apparently done so once, by telegram, and they had been escorted out of the country and banned from returning for a minimum of ten years. The Queen always had the best intentions at heart, but she was only human. No one was perfect, including her. I, for one, would never dare cross her. If any child or parent was disrespectful or broke too many rules, they would be sent away. That had been made very clear to us. If that happened to anyone, they would be welcomed back after ten years, as a one-time courtesy. If any of the adults were asked to leave England due to disrespect or not following the rules, we were all told they would have to take their children with them, because by law, they would not have the right to tell a parent their children must stay. However, if the Queen determined a parent unfit, any child of theirs would be required to stay. The parent could either legally fight to get custody of their child back, or they could sign the rights to their child over to the Palace, and would not be allowed to see them until they reached eighteen years of age. The Queen ruled over all. She could ever overrule any judge's decision. After all, she had extreme power as the Queen of England.

Once I read most of the itinerary, it was time to go to the salon. Once we all gathered there, the maid in charge explained everything I had read on the itinerary. "Sign on your own behalf," she said, after she had explained everything. "If anyone wishes to leave now, then please raise your hand." Some of the teenagers looked angry because they had either tattoos or body piercings, or both. The children seemed happy though, because they only had the one tattoo of Whiskers the kitten, like me. None of us with that tattoo wanted to keep it. We didn't want any reminders of the Evil Bearded Bee Man, as we were all trying to move on and forget. No one raised their hand. "Very well then," said the maid. "Follow me to the salon and let's make you all pure again. The Queen says, 'art should be looked at in pictures at a museum, but not on a human body'. You may not like this change now, but maybe you will be thankful once your memories of them fade, and you can't remember what they used to look like."

All the parents and their children followed her to the salon. All the female children had their ears pierced with pretty diamond earrings. Every single adult and most of the teenagers had at least a few tattoos removed. They weren't too happy about getting an ultimatum. After all, no one would be happy about that. I think they were all concerned about how much the Palace planned on changing everyone. After all, they were the parents of their own children, even if some were unfit. They wondered if these people planned on being the bosses of everyone, all the time. They had provided us all with more than most people could ever dream of, yes. But, would these people become uncontrollable control freaks? Were they going to make us feel like we're under their thumbs, constantly? It had only been one day. So, I decide to wait and see what the next day was like. *Perhaps the Queen won't have too many demands,* I thought. *To meet her will be an honor, so maybe she just needs to give us time to look like and act like we are royalty.* That would be a big change from the ghetto of Union City, New Jersey. *I hope her workers have patience. They were certainly going to need it.*

As we waited our turn in the salon, I thought about the bully, Sam, and if she deserved to be there as well. But, I didn't want to be fighting with her every day. I knew I needed to make a good impression. It was going to be hard, changing from rags to riches. But, I needed to make the best out of this opportunity. I wanted to make something of my life. *My* God had brought me and the others there for a reason. We may have all gone through the worst life experiences to get there, but we were there and I intended to make the best of it. No one in the Bible who I was aware of, had lived a good life, so maybe we were born to struggle, for the purpose of helping each other. I loved to help people and try and make them smile. I usually succeeded too, because I could be really silly. I was also a klutz and had made many people laugh, because I tended to stumble and fall down a lot. They may have laughed at my expense, but making people laugh always made me happy. It still does. Bruises go away, but some bad memories stay in your mind, forever.

5 FAST FORWARD TO 2019

As I explained in Chapter One, this is my first book and I hope it is successful. The truth is, I was just about to wrap it up and write an ending that may or may not have a second part. I was going to make it a short story, but I have too much of an imagination so it may have a second part. But, I'll see how this first book does. I'm learning as I go, as being a writer is new to me. I would love to write full-time, but I first need to see if I have what it takes. I am writing this book from my point of view, as a five-year-old in 1977. But, in reality, it's now the year 2019 and we have smartphones, self-driving cars, Google, Instagram, Facebook, Twitter, et cetera.

I am now fast-forwarding to 2019; how life was in England, living near Buckingham Palace, and I'm thinking of some sort of twist. I'm glad I can make things up as I go along. I am very spontaneous and tend to go with the flow. I hope you, the reader, can have patience with me, as my sorry ass has no idea what I am going to write about next. I hope you also have a sense of humor. I wonder if I will have critics? That would be so cool! I would love for a professional critic to tell me I suck at this. I hope you feel as excited as I do, to find out how this book will end, or if there will be second part. Will I have to throw in the towel as a writer, because I only end up with a handful of readers? I can't wait to find out. But, it's safe to say I am not going to practice signing autographs. Lol

But first, some history… After I had written quite a bit of this book, I messaged a stranger online and asked her a question. We'll call her "Emma".

Messaging a stranger isn't my style. I never private message anyone, except my friends. She is a living kidney donor, and I told her I am also a kidney donor, and was working on writing my first book. I told her I had written a lot of pages, and asked for her advice. She responded, in part:

"Laura, it doesn't really matter how many pages you've written. What matters more is how many words you have written. For a novel, it should be a bare minimum of forty thousand words." Sometimes, learning something new each day can be disappointing. I had a lot more to write, to meet that minimum. When she agreed to help me with this book, I asked her if I could mention her in the acknowledgements, but she didn't want me to. Two less words to worry about. Lol. She wouldn't allow me to use her real name, because she doesn't want any type of credit. That made me think, *Oh crap. Maybe she doesn't want her name in my book because it may be the worst book ever.* I get a bit insecure when I have no clue what I am doing, or if I think I may be wasting my time. But, she assured me she never takes credit for any editing or proofing she does for free on the side, because she doesn't want credit for simply helping someone else. Emma and I are members of an online support group, for living kidney donors. There are thousands of members in our group, and out of everyone there, I chose to send a private message to her. Like I said, I never private message anyone except people I know, but in this case, I believe *my* God made us chat. I wrote to her, "I donated my kidney to stranger as well, and I applaud you." I asked Emma what she did for a living, and she wrote back that she works in the legal field, and is a professional editor. On the side, she spends her extra time volunteering to help new writers finish and publish their first books as e-books, and helps them promote their books online. I said, "Wow, what are the odds I would find someone to help me with my book this quickly?" I wondered why I had told her I was writing a book, and how would I even know what she did for a living? What were the odds of that? It was then, that donating my kidney felt like a big deal, because I wouldn't have ever met Emma online if I hadn't. That took a while to hit me: that I helped save a stranger's life. It felt good. God is good.

I was happy to give up my spare kidney. Plenty of people are born with only one kidney and they're fine. My take on it was, I never created a life, so why not try and save a life? I asked Emma another question, "I am working on a book; would you help me?" She said, "Yes, and at no charge since we are both kidney donors." This part of the story is nonfiction. Both Emma and I really did donate our spare kidneys to strangers.

At the beginning of my kidney donation journey, I was pretty much homeless at the time, and had read on Facebook that a friend of a friend needed a kidney. My friend, Diana Steele, is the one who posted about it. Her husband, Bobby Steele, used to be in a band by the name of, *The Misfits*. But, now they have a new band called, *The Undead*. Diana and Bobby tour with the band, and have a huge following. I am proud of them both.

Diana's Facebook post explained that her friend, Dino, needed a kidney transplant as soon as possible, because he had reached the maximum time to be on dialysis. He also wanted to live long enough to be able to meet his unborn grandson. I am a very spontaneous person and I love to help others. So, without giving it much thought, I asked her for his contact information. I wear hearing aids because I have ringing in both ears, so I said, "Let's text only." After texting with him, I agreed to a simple blood test to see if I was a match for him, and I was. It was then I went through major testing, and eventually did the transplant. It was time consuming and painful, but I had nothing better to do. At the time, people made more of a big deal about it than I did. I was like, "Okay, whatever."

The hospital put me through tons of testing. CT scans, MRIs, bloodwork. I had to pee into a container for twenty-four hours, and bring it to the next state the following day. For some reason, that urine test did not work, so I had to do it again. I had to see a gynecologist to get every single test they had. I pretty much took every test in the book. I ended up being approved as healthy enough to donate, which surprised me. I didn't think I would be healthy enough to do it. I was not the type of person who ate right or exercised. I did quite the opposite. I drank beer, smoked pot and cigarettes and ate a lot of fast food. The hospital told me first that I was a match, before they told Dino, in case I wanted to change my mind about donating to him. Some of my friends and family members thought it was a good idea, others not so much, but it was my decision. The timing was perfect, because I didn't have a job at the time. It was my choice, not theirs.

Someone asked me, what if one of my family members needed a kidney in the future. I answered that question with a question, "What if a kid were drowning next to my boat, but I only had one life raft? Am I to keep that life raft, just in case one of my family members go overboard?"

That person said, "Good answer," and smiled.

When I found out I was approved to donate to Dino, I called him up and told him we were a match, and the surgery would be in January unless he was too busy. Dino, this big tough man, cried tears of joy. It was hard for me to hear him cry. They were tears of joy and gratitude. He was speechless, so I told him, "Get your words together and call me later." I admit, I hesitated on whether I should choose to be listed as an organ donor on my driver's license, but I checked the 'yes' box. Having them remove one of my kidneys while I was still alive? That made me think it over. But I decided I would do it, regardless of the risks. I really liked the hospital staff at New York Presbyterian hospital in New York City. The Sergeant had done thousands of transplants, so I knew I was in good hands. After weeks of waiting for Dino to be healthy enough for the transplant surgery, surgery day finally arrived. The ride into New York City took so long due to traffic. When we arrived, we were both put in our hospital gowns. We were then allowed to talk to each other before the transplant.

I reminded Dino they were giving him my right kidney, which had a cyst on it. Maybe he had forgotten, or hadn't heard me when I had told him weeks before. He asked, "What are they going to do, remove the cyst before they give me the kidney?" I told him I didn't know, and had forgotten to ask, but I figured he could find out if he wanted to. He sighed.

"Hey," I said to him. "If you're not happy with the merchandise, you can go to elevator C, and take it to the fourth floor. Make your first right, then make a left and you will see a complaints department right past the water fountain." A nurse overheard me and laughed.

Dino smiled, and the nurse pushed his bed to the right, mine to the left, and we said, "We got this!" Dino was once a stranger, but is now a very good friend of mine. I didn't remember anything about the actual surgery. When I woke up from the anesthesia, I was in a private room. There was a TV and a window. I was as high as a kite and wasn't feeling any pain, so I wrote on Facebook that the surgery had been successful, but I hadn't yet heard from Dino. I needed to know if his body had accepted my kidney. I saw that people were posting to him on Facebook, but he had not replied to anyone. I called his phone, but got his voicemail. I called his wife. No answer. I then pushed the button for the nurse, and she came right in. She said, "You woke up. How do you feel?" I ignored the question and asked how Dino was. She said, "He is sleeping, but neither of you had any complications. You should rest for now. In a few hours, I would like for you to get up and walk around. It will be difficult, but it's mandatory. It will help prevent blood clots and relieve some gas."

I was so out of it from the meds, I said, "Okay, you're a good 'nursey'."

She said, "Push the button if you need anything at all."

I said, "Thank you, nursey-nursey-nursey friend." She giggled and left the room. I fell asleep the second I took out my contacts. A few hours later, I felt so much pain I pushed the IV button for pain medication to release into my bloodstream. Since the anesthesia had worn off, I was really uncomfortable in my own skin. I didn't want to talk to or see anyone. I looked out the hospital window and wanted to jump to my death due to the pain. I wasn't suicidal, but the pain was unbearable. Even though the IV button worked pretty fast, the pain meds hadn't kicked in yet. Then, I thought of how stupid the headlines would look, and what people would think: *Woman, 45 Years Old, Saves a Stranger's Life By Donating Her Kidney To Him And Then Jumps Out Window To Her Death.* If I had read something like that, I would think that person was pathetic. I rolled my eyes at myself. I tried to fall asleep and as soon as I finally did, the nurse woke me up. She said I needed to walk, but my body didn't want to move.

"Okay," I said. "Can I sleep for an hour or two, first? My body is aching." She agreed, and I slept until she woke me up again. I still felt the same, so I told her I would walk later.

She said, "Nope. You can get a blood clot if you don't walk. In addition, it will relieve some gas and that will make you feel better." It took all my might to get up out of bed. It was so weird to have a catheter and not be able to feel it when I urinated. I found that awkward. It took all the energy I had to get up and hold onto the walker. I took baby steps, as I held on to my IV pole. The nurses were telling me what a good job I was doing. I didn't have any visitors, because as I mentioned before, the transplant took place in New York City. It was only the next state over, but I had requested no visitors. I did have one great friend, Kevin Carney, try to visit me. But, I sent him away. I didn't want to see anyone at all. Plus, the gas and tolls to get there from New Jersey were outrageous. I just took baby steps and kept walking. It did help relieve some of the gas pains. I kept on going longer than required. That's the Jersey girl in me. Jersey girls are tough and do not pump gas. In the hallway, there were signs of how far you had walked. I went about a mile or so, and then went back to my room. I instantly fell asleep and was woken up three hours later to take a sleeping pill. That made zero sense, but I fell back asleep. I was there two more days before I was released.

At one point, my niece texted me a picture of my dog, Dakota, that she had taken. Dakota looked like she was praying. The text said Dakota hadn't been herself since I left. Me and my Dakota have a bond that's nearly as strong as the bond I had with Oreo. We spend so much time together. I made her a service dog, so she can accompany me anywhere in public, no questions asked. She has her service vest harness and identification. I couldn't wait until I could go home to her! I really don't like hospitals, but the staff was very friendly. I never opened the bag I packed for the hospital stay. I never watched the TV. All I wanted to do was sleep. The only annoying thing was, the nurses woke me up every three hours, so I couldn't wait to get out of there and finally have some uninterrupted sleep.

At 6:00 a.m. sharp one morning, the nurse told me that after I ate my breakfast I had to walk. I said, "Okay, but today is the day I get to leave. What time can I go?"

She said, "Probably later this evening. The anesthesia can sometimes cause a person's bowels to go to sleep. You just need to have a bowel movement, so we are sure they're awake and working properly before you are discharged. After you do that, the surgeon will see you and then discharge you." I asked for some coffee. I knew that was the best laxative for me. When my coffee arrived, I looked at the breakfast. The package said it was eggs but that wasn't eggs! It was something I couldn't identify. I'm the pickiest eater ever, and there was no way I was going to eat whatever that was. I just downed my coffee and walked, so they wouldn't nag me to do it.

I was a difficult person at times. I don't like rules, and I certainly don't like being told what to do by anyone. Even more now, than when I was a kid. I was determined to go home, so after about a half hour of walking, I went back to my room's private toilet and refused to get up until I had moved my bowels. It only took twenty minutes. I knew the nurse needed to see the proof before I would be released, so I didn't flush it. When the nurse came in, I showed her the bathroom and nicely asked if I could see the doctor and be discharged. She agreed. I don't wait well, so after two hours of sitting in my room wanting to get out of there, I took the IV out myself. I ripped the tape off fast, like a Band-Aid and took the needle out. Oops… There was blood, so I took a cotton ball and applied pressure. Then, put the tape back on. I had experience with needles, due to my junky parents. Until then, I had been satisfied with my experience in that hospital. But, I ended up having to wait eight hours to be discharged, so I was pretty mad. Then, my pre-arranged ride canceled on me at the last minute, due to car trouble. A staff member from the hospital carpool department came and got me, in a wheelchair, and rolled me and my bag to my recipient's hospital room.

Dino, my recipient, was on a different floor. It was the first time I had seen him since the transplant. I asked him how *our* kidney was doing, and he looked at me and started crying tears of joy. That was the second time I had seen a grown man cry.

The first time was when I had to take my dog to the vet to be put to sleep, due to old age. My brother-in-law cried, and he's not a crier. It was one of the saddest moments of my life. Oh, how I still miss Oreo. She was a great doggie, my BFF. When I left England, Oreo and I moved back to the United States and into my sister's home where Oreo became the family dog. My sister hadn't liked England, so she had moved back to the United States, married and had children: my niece and nephew, Kerri and Jason. I love them all. Oreo and I lived in their basement for a while, and my sister, brother-in-law and the kids all got attached to Oreo.

I hope to never witness a grown man's tears again. It makes me cry. Dino, my recipient, was at a loss for words, and thanked me as he was lying in his hospital bed. He said so many nice things to me, with tears in his eyes, but I cut him off because I wanted to get home. I was still in a lot of pain. I asked him if he could get me a ride home because my ride had cancelled. "Anything for you!" he said. The hospital carpool lady hadn't been willing to wait five minutes, so I could talk to Dino, and figure out how I was getting home. She had left me in his room, in the middle of a question I was asking her. What a bitch. People like her shouldn't work in a place where patients need empathy, especially after they've had major surgery. So, once Dino had ordered a car for me, I had to wait for a hospital carpool person to come back. I had really liked that hospital in the beginning, but getting out of there took forever. After talking to Dino for a while, the car he got for me was on its way, so I needed to leave ASAP. The car service would charge five dollars for every ten minutes they had to wait. The hospital carpool was late of course, so I wrote a strongly-worded letter to the hospital. I received a refund and free parking vouchers, which I gave them to Dino for his follow-up visits. I had told the hospital I wouldn't be afraid to Yelp, even though I had no idea how to do that. But, they obviously cared about their online ratings, so they went above and beyond to accommodate me. They even said they would fire the carpool worker, but I asked them not to, to please give her a warning. I would hate to be responsible for somebody losing their income. The cost of living is very expensive and it's hard to keep your head above water.

Once the hospital carpool person finally showed up and took me out to the car waiting for me, I was headed home to Dumont, New Jersey. I felt bad leaving my recipient's room so quickly. The poor guy has to take about thirty-six pills each day, and deal with so much expense to go into New York City from his home in New Jersey, for medical follow-ups. He also had to stay in the hospital for at least a week longer than I did. I was told to just lower my cholesterol by eating better (yeah, right like I'm going to do that). They also told me to drink eight glasses of water a day, which I do. One beer, one glass of water, et cetera. I have my kidney levels checked annually, and so far, so good. Like I said, I am Jersey tough.

I was forty-five years old when I donated my kidney, and twenty-two years old when I had my heart broken for the first time. I had left England when I turned eighteen, to move back to the United States. I had fallen crazy in love with a musician, who had told me he was unhappily married. He was my everything. I lived to please him. I thought about him from the second I woke up until the moment I fell asleep every night. My goal in life, which I believed was his also, was for us to be together, once his child was old enough for college. He would tell me how it was going to be just me and him one day, and how great things would be once he was coming home to me. I was in love, young and very dumb. Please, try not to judge me. No one is perfect and I know now that I was addicted to him. I was also suffering from depression and anxiety. He was my life at the time. I stayed with him on and off for two decades. Oh, how I looked the other way and believed everything he told me, for over twenty years. I'm ashamed to admit it, but to be closer to him, I also managed to become friends with his wife, and babysat for their son. Talk about obsession! I was beyond obsessed. He would say jump, and I'd ask how high? He would say shit, and I'd ask what flavor? I thought with my heart, instead of my head.

His wife caught us together one day, and I backed off a lot. I lost myself to pot and alcohol, but I still refused to let him go. I stayed with him, even though I knew he was not only cheating on his wife, but was cheating on me as well. I didn't know how to let him go, because he was the only life I had known for my entire adult life. I fought to be with him with all my might. I won't blame him for everything though, because I was no angel.

Eventually though, the worst thing that could happen to me and my heart, did happen. I found out, as I was allowing him to string me along, that he was getting divorced and had already moved in with some chick he had met less than a year before. I found all that out on Facebook, and I saw *red*. It was then that I finally wanted zero to do with him, after I made a huge scene in front of him and his band members. I screamed at him and he got a bouncer to kick me out, as if I was out of line, even though I was reacting like anyone would, if they learned they had been led on and lied to by someone for over twenty years.

I was so angry, I decided to tell his wife and I did. I also gave her my most sincere apologies. She pretty much forgave me, as fully as she could. She knew it was his fault much more than mine. We had both been lied to by the same man, for years, but she had an entire life with him. She was fifteen years older than me and they had a child together. She believed they would be a family forever. When she said she felt as if her entire life had been a lie, I could relate to that. She said she had picked the wrong guy. I ended up being friends with her again, as we sadly had a lot in common. I gave her a lot of credit for forgiving me, and I knew it would get back to the musician in time. I don't want to mention his real name, so I'll call him 'Bruce'.

Later, when I was almost done crying over him, I went to a bar to see his band play. I hadn't seen him in a while, but I had spent half my life with him, so I still loved him. I could tell he was sad, but at the same time, happy to see me. He told me the gal he had left me for, the one he had moved in with, was sick and in the hospital. After a few drinks, guess who I went home with? Yup, I fell back in love with him and we had amazing sex that night. I hated myself in the morning. I hated myself for letting him control me again. We started dating again, and I hung on his every word, once again. I was such an idiot for taking him back, and had no dignity or pride left. He stayed with the sick gal because she was sick, and I ended up fighting with her over him because she heard a message I had left, after she was released from the hospital. I was 'the other woman', *again.*

What the fuck was wrong with me? Why couldn't I just walk away, once and for all? Why did I still love him, after everything he had put me through? "Here we go again," I thought, as he told me how we were 'meant to be' and we would be together one day. I was mad at myself for still wanting that future with him. His attitude was pretty much, 'not everything goes as planned'. I loved him and hated him at the same time, and I felt like a horrible friend to his wife. It was hard to look at myself in the mirror, and one day I had the guts to confess to her that I was with him again. I went through a deep depression, after I told her about me and him. I don't know why he still had such power over me. Why did I allow myself to become 'the other woman', *again?*

The sick gal he was with ended up becoming even sicker, and then suddenly passed away. I hadn't wished her dead, of course. But, I admit I hadn't wished her well, either. After she died, he was the grieving boyfriend, even acting as if I didn't exist, at times. I looked the other way, as he posted online about how his life was 'in pieces without her'. Then, he would call me and say how much he needed me. So, of course, I went running right back to him again. For every negative thing I have to say about him, I have three positive things to say. It was the strangest love-hate relationship, ever. At that time, I believed, "He's not letting me go, so maybe we are meant for each other!" I was such a sucker.

We both came from lives where our parents hadn't done a very good job of raising their kids. We understood what most people do not. Within one year of his girlfriend's death, the bastard did it to me again. He moved in with some rich sugar mama, who was madly head-over-heels for her little boy-toy. Talk about history repeating itself. That to, I found out through social media. And, they ended up getting engaged. Fucking asshole. I truly hated him after I saw they were planning to get married. I wasn't answering his calls, and was done. Yeah, right. I finally answered and told him how hurt I was. After talking, I decided to allow him to stay in my life as a friend. We had helped each other out for so many years, and I needed his help. It was a love-hate relationship, but I knew I would always love him no matter what. I really should seek help.

I did say some mean things. Bittersweet revenge. I said something to him like, "Have fun marring someone who looks like a grandmother." I know that pissed him off, because he's sensitive when it comes to age. I also called them 'the gruesome twosome', on social media, and he blocked me. I am fourteen years younger than him, and she looks much older than him. I told him not to even think about calling me for a 'booty call'. Who did he think he was, messing with my head and heart for *so long*.

As I was writing this book, I received a text from a mutual friend. It was a picture of his wedding invitation. His very smart and talented daughter was in the wedding. I thought I could at least try to make a clean break from him. But, I loved him too much to let go, and needed him emotionally and financially. I was not using him, because we have always helped each other over the years. His ex-wife, who amazingly forgave me, will always have ties to him, whether she wants to or not, because they have a kid together. Yet, I kept going back for more, willingly. I was obsessed. I really should have seen a psychiatrist. The wedding invitation had their address on it, and the date and time of the wedding. I wondered if I should try and ruin their wedding day, since I felt like he had ruined my life. I had four weeks to decide.

I have a close friend who has connections to a few motorcycle gangs, including the Hell's Angels. He told me to call him if I ever needed anything at all. I wondered if I should have them crash the wedding, but I didn't have the guts to ask. I wouldn't have asked anyway, because people could have been hurt and I don't have a violent bone in my body. I'm all talk. I did, however, think of playing that card as a final goodbye to him. Like, *checkmate.* Revenge is fun to think about, even if you know you won't do anything.

I still love him and we still help each other, but we just have a different relationship now. I work for him sometimes, too. It's hard to work for an ex, but we keep it professional as I stress over money. The day I wrote this was August 28, 2018 and his wedding date was September 29, 2018. Karma would sure have to do a number on that boy. I did fantasize about crashing his wedding, and then going home and singing *Friends in Low Places,* with a bottle of wine. I so went back and forth on that one.

That's another exciting part about writing. I really didn't know at that point, what I would do. I sat there writing this book, thinking, "I won't know what will happen until the day of his wedding, four weeks and one day from now. So, you the reader, and I, really are clueless as to what will happen." I still wasn't sure if I should try and ruin his "black tie affair", but without hurting anyone. I was looking at the photo of the invitation, and it read in large print, "At last". At last? Are you fucking kidding me? They had been together for less than a year, and he had strung me along for decades. "At last," I said to myself, shaking my head. It was more like, "Already? Too soon!" It also read, "Hope you will make this memory with them", and I thought, "Hmm... They are asking for it. They want a memory? Oh, it's in black and white, in writing." Lol – "They are making my decision easier," I thought. In my defense, I could always say, "Their invitation said 'hope you will make this memory with them', so I *did.* Duh, what's the problem?" Ah, but his bride will learn the hard way that she'll have to share her boy toy with other women. A leopard never changes its spots.

Once a cheater, always a cheater, et cetera. I never got any revenge, and I maintain a friendship with him. He helped me out of a financial mess and I do love the guy. Yes, I know, I need to get my head examined. My heart is in the right place, though. We sometimes work together, but he keeps it in his pants. At least, with me. But, we do kiss on the rare occasions we see each other, and I tell him I love him, because I really do. I vent a lot to all my friends, which I'm sure he isn't happy about. He hates drama, although he creates it. I do love a lot of people and I was taught to never burn bridges, no matter what. Love really does suck sometimes, though. But, I have taught myself to let things go, and let Karma or *my* God fight my battles. It's hard to do, because I am impatient, and Karma sometimes takes too long.

Speaking of Karma, it did finally catch up with the Evil Bearded Bee Man.

6 CHECKMATE

The Evil Bearded Bee Man's lawyer was able to get his charges dropped down to only rape, meaning he got away with the 'multiple murders'. The prosecution hadn't been able to prove Joseph Gonzalez had any part in the 'mass killing', so he was only sentenced to fifteen years for the multiple rape charges. The Queen wasn't at all satisfied with his sentencing. It did not sit well with her, and I had never seen her so angry. It was as if she had a personal vendetta against him. She constantly spoke about getting revenge against him, once he was released from jail. And, what the Queen wanted, the Queen got. I remember it like it was yesterday.

It was all over the news that, based on good behavior, the Evil Bearded Bee Man had been released from prison after only doing fifteen years, only a matter of months for each child he had traumatized. His lawyer had certainly worked for that $2,500-per-hour. He even raised his hourly rate, after defending the Evil Bearded Bee Man. He knew with his new reputation for helping people get away with murder, the people who needed his services would pay top dollar. So, he set his new rate at $3,500-per-hour, and was fully booked in weeks. That lawyer's net worth went sky high in a short period of time, so the Queen was pissed.

I learned my lesson the hard way, to never piss off the Queen. A few months after the Evil Bearded Bee Man's trial ended, his high-priced lawyer was murdered, and it remains unsolved. He was despised by many, for defending the most hated man on earth. It was possible that even President Carter could have been behind the lawyer's murder, since the lawyer had never cooperated with any requests. That lawyer had only cared about *money*, nothing else. Some greedy, stingy people need to learn the lesson that, when you die, you don't take your money with you. The lawyer hadn't ever figured out all the 'murder victims' were still alive, so that was a relief.

When I lived in the Queen's backyard, I figured out a way to sneak out, and went out and got drunk. I was only fifteen years old. The look she gave me and the distance she put between us, after she learned I had been caught sneaking back in, certainly taught me a lesson. It felt as if she had taken away her love, and that hurt. It took months of me kissing her ass, to get it back. When I got her to start liking me again, I held on tight and we eventually became closer than ever before. She didn't make it easy, though. But, she ended up taking very good care of all of us girls who had been victims in the Underground Fort rape case. She treated us as if we were her daughters. We were disciplined, but very spoiled by her, and her love was like no other. I thought she wanted revenge so badly against the Evil Bearded Bee Man, because he had raped 'her girls'. But, it turned out, she had a personal vendetta toward the Evil Bearded Bee Man. About ten years after we had all arrived in England as young girls, Joseph Gonzalez was released early from prison, having only served nine of his fifteen-year sentence. Immediately, the Queen had a team of her people travel to the United States to get him and bring him back. Less than twenty-four hours after his release from prison, he appeared in front of her in handcuffs, with a guard on each side of him. She called all of us girls to Buckingham Palace, immediately, to join them.

Oh, how I will *never* forget that day, the day I saw the Queen's evil, revengeful smile. I remember it like it was yesterday. She had us all stand outside the room he was in, and handed us each a large empty cup. We were all between the ages of fifteen and eighteen years old, at that time. There were several full buckets of what looked like honey.

"Now, gather around ladies," she said. "Today is the day I've been waiting for, for a *very* long time." As she paced in front of us, she spoke loudly, "I hereby declare today a national holiday, and it shall be called 'Karma Day'." The Queen had the power to do whatever she wanted to do in England. She continued, "Behind this door is the man who raped you, and took away your innocence. He does not know you girls are alive, so I can't wait to see his face when he sees all of you. Unless…" She looked at all of us carefully. "If any of you do not wish to be in the same room with him, that's perfectly alright. I assure you. Please raise your hand if you would rather be excused." Four girls raised their hands. "Very well. Our meeting with him will be recorded on video, if any of you would like to watch it later, darlings. You're excused." The four of them left quickly. Their faces made it clear they still feared the man. The remaining twenty-one of us, however, couldn't wait to see him. We wanted the chance to confront him, especially to show him he hadn't broken us. My heart raced as I looked at the door to the room. He was on the other side of it. I felt excited as I thought about what I would say to him.

"When you see him," the Queen said, "he will be securely tied up, so he won't be able to hurt any of you." She smiled reassuringly, and looked at the buckets. "In honor of the swarm of honeybees that attacked this man, allowing Laura to escape from him, thankfully," she said as she smiled at me, "I decided *honey* would be the perfect thing for each of you to greet him with today. As I'm sure you know, honey is very thick. Therefore, these buckets are full of honey mixed with water, so it's much thinner. Each of you will have the opportunity to approach him separately. I would like for you to pour your honey on him, or throw your honey at him, whatever you prefer… and say what you would like to say to him; anything you'd like. Alright?" We all agreed. "Any questions?" she asked. I spoke up and asked the Queen if we could all take our turns in the order of 'our circle', the circle we had created so many years before, at the ice-skating rink. I explained to the Queen that ever since then, we had always sat in the same order when in our circle, even in our weekly group therapy sessions.

The Queen smiled. "Of course, my dear Laura. That sounds perfectly lovely," she said in a motherly tone of voice. It was the tone I loved the most. I really looked up to her, as if she were my real mother. I had called her 'mom' once, but she had quickly corrected me. She had insisted I never call her anything except, 'Your Majesty'. It was even disrespectful for anyone to refer to her as 'Queen', when speaking directly to her. I was hurt, but had obeyed her wish, for I knew better than to ever break any rules again. I didn't want to end up in the royal doghouse, ever again. The Queen would get upset if one of us simply held our tea cup incorrectly, so you can only imagine the look in her eyes when she confronted me about calling her 'mom'. I had always been 'the good one', so I felt like I had let her down.

"The moment has finally arrived," the Queen said loudly, and she turned and opened the double doors. I knew once we walked through those doors, we would all be facing the man who had stolen our innocence. We grabbed each other's hands and walked in, hand-in-hand. The Queen had ordered the Evil Bearded Bee Man to stand in the center of the room with a few guards, and with her. His hands were tied in front of him, and his feet were chained. Two guards stood behind him, and one on each side, each holding one of his arms. As the Queen walked toward him to take her place, we all formed a wide circle around him.

He no longer had a beard. Dozens of prison tattoos covered his skin, even his face. There wasn't one place on his body that wasn't covered with ink. He looked around the circle, confused, and then asked the Queen, "What in bloody hell's name is going on here? For fuck's sake, who are these brats?"

"First," the Queen began in a firm voice. "These fine young ladies are not *brats,* and I strongly suggest you refrain from disrespecting them any further, *especially* in *my* presence. Is that clear?" He grunted in response, and the Queen continued, staring directly into his eyes. "Second, I am very pleased to inform you, these women are some of the *innocent* young girls you forced your penis into without their permission. Remember?" She smiled sweetly at him, enjoying every second.

His eyes widened. "That's preposterous, for they are all dead!" he yelled.

Upon hearing that, the Queen laughed, and said, "Ah, good point. One would think that, wouldn't they? But, you are mistaken, Joseph. They are all very much alive and well, as you can see." You could never underestimate the Queen's power, and what she was capable of. The Queen started to sing, "For I, with a little help from my friends…" We all laughed. We had never heard the Queen sing, or ever seen her so happy before. We also laughed because we knew, "living well is the best revenge", and we had certainly lived well. The Queen then continued in her speaking voice, "I succeeded in convincing the entire world they were all dead, and I've waited for this moment for many years." She turned toward all of us girls and smiled. "But, this isn't *my* moment. It belongs to these strong young women." The Queen turned and glared at him. "Ladies," she called out. "He is all yours." She then took a few steps back, and waited to watch us deal with him.

I called out loudly as I walked toward him, "Thank you, Your Majesty!" I was standing right in front of him within a few seconds and focused only on *him*. "Hello there, *Un*bearded Evil Bearded Bee Man," I said. "I am the one and only Buttercup!" His eyes went small, squinting at me, before going really wide as he recognized me. *I can't wait to see this on camera later*, I thought. He stared at me.

"No way…" he mumbled.

"Way…" I said. "Now, speak *not*!" I ordered him loudly, as I splashed my cup of watered-down honey all over his face. He cringed. Oh, how good it felt to be in control of this evil man. I looked at the Queen. Her smile was from ear to ear, and she winked at me. I smiled and winked back, then continued. "I no longer go by thy name 'Buttercup', for my name is Laura May. You may have thought you won, but losers never win. We beat you, and today is so not going to be a good day for you. I and my crew are going to show you what revenge feels like! What doesn't kill you makes you stronger. For we have our whole lives ahead of us, and thanks to the Queen, our future is brighter than the sun. For you don't have one, as today will be the day you *die*!" I assumed the Queen wouldn't let him live. "Have fun in hell!" I yelled, as I turned from him and skipped back to the circle, over to Lisa. We both jumped into the air as our palms connected in a high-five. Lisa then joyfully smiled as she skipped to the middle of the circle, ready to take her turn with the Evil *Un*Bearded Bee Man.

"Hi, I'm Lisa. When I was six-and-a-half years old, I was one of the two gals you raped up the ass! It was an entrance, not an exit! I was saving myself for marriage, but at least I can save my vagina for my future husband! I am now seventeen years old, and two men have *not* demanded, but have requested me to do the same thing. One of them was my boyfriend. I said yes, and was great at it. I turned your negative into a positive. I've heard he's going to propose to me one day. You didn't do good, but I made it into good. I have pet bees now, and they remind me of how the bees tortured you, like you have tortured too many innocent children. You're a waste product!" she yelled, as she threw her cup of honey at his crotch, hard. She skipped away smiling, just like I had done, as the man bent over in pain. The guard behind him grabbed him by the shoulders and with a quick elbow to his back, forced him to stand up straight. Emma was next.

"Hi, my name is Emma. I am seventeen years old. You took away my virginity when I was only six-and-a-half years old. Shame on you! I was the second gal whose exit you used as an entrance. You gave us all the sick souvenirs of the tattoo of Whiskers, but just so you know, the Queen had them all removed! Also, the police gave me another of your sick souvenirs, my underwear. But, you can have them back now." She quickly soaked the underwear in her cup of honey and then shoved them tightly into his mouth. He grunted and choked a bit as Emma did a cartwheel, and then skipped back to her place in the circle. Next up was Jamie.

"Hi, I'm Jamie, and I'm fifteen years old now. I was only five years old when you raped me. I still have nightmares. Because of you hitting me in the head when I ran from you, I now have hearing loss in both ears and wear hearing aids. I only wanted a kitten." She quietly poured her cup of honey over his head, and then walked back to the circle. Katie walked up to him next.

"Hi, I am Katie. I was only four-and-a-half years old when you kidnapped me at an amusement park, when I couldn't find my mommy. You told me you knew where she was, but that was a lie. You made me have sex with you, you *sicko*. I wish you had never been born. I never go to amusement parks because of you." She poured her cup of honey into his lap and then looked at him for a long few seconds, until he looked up at her. The moment he made eye contact, she spit in his face, turned and jogged back to the circle. Alexus smiled at her as she passed her, on her way to have her turn with the man.

"Hi, I am Alexus. I was only four-and-a-half years old when you came through my bedroom window and put duct tape over my mouth, so I couldn't scream for help. It was dark at your underground fort and I was so scared. Unlike the other girls, you didn't even offer me a kitten. But, you did put that kitten tattoo on my butt. I'm glad it's gone, and I don't even remember what it looked like. When you let me go after you were done with me, it was too dark for me to find my way home. So, I had to sleep under a tree until the sun came up. It was so cold, and I ended up with pneumonia, as well as Lyme disease from a tick bite I got that night. I still have lung issues, as well as symptoms from the Lyme. But, I'm still glad you didn't get the death penalty, because the Queen has a *much better* punishment awaiting you." His eyes got wide as she poured her cup of honey all around his shoulders and neck. Then, she did a perfect backflip, flipped him the bird as she landed, smiled and walked back toward the circle.

"Right on," Victoria said with a smile, as she passed her. She was next to take her turn. "Hi, my name is Victoria. I was five years old when you pulled my pants down. I said, "*No!* Please stop." But, since you're a disgusting monster, not worth the oxygen you breathe, you said 'no' and told me I would like it. That was a lie, and I am sure you will regret that." She poured her cup of honey over his face, surprising him and causing him to gag again, the sounds of his gagging muffled by Emma's underwear, still stuffed into his mouth. Victoria walked back to the circle. Vicky was next, and stared him down as she walked toward him.

"Hi, my name is Vicky. I wanted to save myself for marriage. You took that away from me! It took a long time for me to speak up, because I didn't think anyone would believe me. I don't even want to be near you. You stink like the piece of crap you are, and you make me sick! She threw her honey cup at him, as she turned to go, and slipped a bit. The cup of honey accidently hit the guard who was protecting the Queen. "I'm so sorry!" Vicky said to the guard. The guard assured her he was alright as he steadied the cup of honey. It hadn't spilled much. She looked at the Queen. "Your Majesty! I'm so sorr—"

"It was an accident," the Queen interrupted. "It's quite alright." Vicky thanked her and turned to walk back to her place in the circle. But, the guard stopped her with a wink and a smile, holding out the nearly-full cup of honey. Vicky smiled back and took it. She turned back to Joseph Gonzalez and looked at him.

"Again, you make me *sick*," she said, and threw the cup of honey at his chest so hard, he grunted as it hit him. Vicky walked back toward the circle as Janet started toward the Evil UnBearded Bee Man.

"Hi, my name is Janet. I was seven years old when you took me out of the girls' bathroom at the zoo. You said if I screamed, you would throw me in the lion's cage. You and your friend thought it was funny when you both raped me repeatedly in your underground fort. Now, I think it's funny it's payback time!" She laughed as she poured her cup of honey over one of his ears, and then the other. The next girl walked up to him, as Janet headed back to her spot.

"Hi, my name is Gloria. I was six years old when you put your private part where it didn't belong. People say I was in the wrong place at the wrong time. I was in the right place, but you weren't. Shame on you!" She started to pour her cup of honey over his eyes. When he tried to put his head down to avoid the honey, the guard behind him grabbed his head and held it up. Gloria thanked the guard. The Evil Unbearded Bee Man started to mumble something to her through his honey-soaked underwear-filled mouth, but the Queen ordered him to remain silent. He reluctantly obeyed. Gloria finished covering his eyes with the honey and then jogged back to the circle, as the next girl walked to where the man stood.

"Hi, my name is Cheryl. You took me from right in front of my own home, as I was playing ball. I wish it would have rained that day, because I would have stayed inside if it had and you wouldn't have even seen me to take me. My nightmares are finally gone now." She poured the honey over his mouth. "I beat you, you know… I beat you by living a rich and happy life, thanks to the authorities and the Queen," she said as she started to walk back toward the circle. "You make us all *sick*, you waste product!" Jackie gave her a high-five as they passed each other.

"Hi, my name is Jackie. I was five-and-a-half years old, exactly. It was my half birthday, when you took so much away from me. Thanks to Laura, I didn't allow you to take my voice though. I didn't let you scare me into not telling on you." She poured the honey over one of his shoulders, and turned and walked back to the circle, smiling at the other girls. Nicole was next.

"Hi, my name is Nicole. I am now sixteen. I tried so hard to forget what you did to me, but I couldn't. I knew in time you would be punished. Your blood money may have saved you years in prison, but it will certainly not save you today." She threw the honey into his face, smiled, and walked away. Jennifer skipped toward him, smiling at Nicole as she passed her.

"Hi, my name is Jennifer. I am now sixteen years old. After you raped me, I turned into a mean child. I did some bad things, but the Queen saved me. I now do nonprofit work, and I help people in need, including people who have been hurt by people like you. You are pure evil." She poured the honey over each of his ears. "It's our turn to watch you suffer," she said, as she skipped away. Cathy smiled as she passed her, walking toward the honey-soaked man.

"Hi, my name is Cathy. I was a nice little girl until you violated me. You created so much change for the worse, for many families. You are a monster, because you enjoyed doing it. I still sleep with a nightlight on, but I won't have to anymore, after today." She poured the honey over both of his arms and skipped away, passing Chelsey with a smile.

"Hi, my name is Chelsey. I was seven years old when you raped me. I used to laugh at everything, but listening to you laugh as you hurt me, took away my sense of humor. Throughout the years, I have found my laughter again. You will never take anything away from anyone, ever again." She poured the honey over his shoulders, as she laughed. It ran down his back. She then hopped away like a bunny rabbit, and a few of the girls giggled. Betty was next.

"Hi, my name is Betty. I was five years old when you raped me, the day my life felt like it turned into a jigsaw puzzle. But, I've put it back together. There was just one piece missing. But, now that you're here, my life is complete, and your life has been in pieces for years. I love that twist." She poured her cup of watered-down honey over both of his tied-up hands, and then walked back to the circle, passing Lucy on the way.

"Hi, my name is Lucy. I am now fifteen years old. I used to fear all men with facial hair, because of your smelly, gross beard. My father shaved his beard off for me, so I would be comfortable around him. But, soon after we came here to England, I told my father he could grow his beard out again, because the Queen made me feel safer than ever. There's no way you're going to heaven, so enjoy hell. I am sure you will fit in well there!" She gave him an evil look, then poured her cup of honey down both of his arms, and went back to the circle, passing Emily on the way back.

"Hi, my name is Emily. You raped me on my seventh birthday. Because of you, I spent my birthday in the hospital. Medicine helps control my panic attacks. I was supposed to be opening presents and blowing out candles. But, today, throwing this cup of honey in your face will be the best present ever. By the way, your daughter Sam will suffer as well. It sucks when people you love get hurt, ay?" He tried to mumble something about not hurting his daughter, but it was incoherent due to his mouth full of souvenir underwear. Emily laughed at him as she threw her cup of honey in his face, and then skipped back to her spot. Lynn gave Emily a high-five as they passed each other.

"We finally meet again," Lynn said with a smile as she stood in front of the man. "I'm Lynn, and I was only four-and-a-half years old when you raped me. You were able to rape me, because I ran away after my mom said I couldn't have chocolate. After I healed from the pain you inflicted, I couldn't stand to even look at chocolate. But, I got over it and now enjoy eating chocolate again." She took two pieces of chocolate from her pocket, each wrapped in silver foil. Would you like a piece?" she asked the man, with a smile. He looked confused. Lynn's smile disappeared. "Hmm, on second thought, evil and disgusting animals like you can't have treats." She smirked at him as she put them back into her pocket. "But, I'm happy to share this sweet honey with you." She reached up above his head and turned her cup of honey upside down, chuckling as it covered his head and shoulders. Then, she turned and walked away, passing Amanda who stopped her and gave her a quick hug and peck on the cheek. Amanda stared daggers at the Evil Unbearded Bee Man as she walked toward him.

"Hi, my name is Amanda. I am now eighteen years old. You raped me when I was a little girl, and just so you know, you sucked at it. I realized that when my high school boyfriend and I made love for the first time. At only sixteen years old, he was more of a man than you ever were. And, that's coming from a lesbian. Yes, I love women. But, that's not a result of what you did to me, but because I was born this way. I shut down emotionally, after you stole my innocence. But, the Queen, and all my friends…" Amanda nodded toward the Queen and motioned to us girls, "my honorary *sisters* that is; they helped me heal, and I realized a long time ago that I deserve to be happy." Amanda turned back to the circle and made eye contact with Lynn. "Come here," Amanda said to her, smiling. Lynn seemed confused, but walked toward her. As Lynn got closer, Amanda suddenly dropped to one knee with a huge smile, and reached into one of her pockets. Lynn squealed and jumped up and down, as Amanda pulled out a diamond ring. Amanda smiled widely and held the ring up to Lynn. "Will you please marry me?" Lynn looked at the ring, totally caught off-guard. The Queen's face dropped.

"Ye-e-e-s!" Lynn yelled in delight, almost knocking Amanda backwards as she fell into her arms. Lynn kissed her on the cheek with a big "Mmm-u-a-h!" Amanda hugged her and slipped the ring onto Lynn's left ring finger. "Oh, my!" Lynn said. Her mouth hung open in shock as she stared at the ring. The rest of the girls yelled out our congratulations, as both Lynn and Amanda stood up. The Queen held up one hand, and everyone quieted down instantly. Amanda turned to look at the pathetic man standing in front of her. "You see, you didn't kill us after all. In fact, if it wasn't for you, we wouldn't be living this incredible life in a palace, and with more money than we could ever hope to spend in our lives. But, you'll never get a thank you from me, or anyone. *This* is for the pain you caused me. May you forever burn in hell." She poured her cup of honey down the front of him. It dripped down both of his legs and onto his feet. She threw the empty cup into his face, turned and kissed her new fiancé, and the two of them walked back to our circle, holding hands. They were the last two girls to speak. All twenty-one of us who had been brave enough to have our say, were finished. I was proud of the twenty-one of us, but sad for the four girls who had chosen not to confront him. I hoped they wouldn't regret it later. I felt better than I had in a long time, and looking around at the others, it appeared they felt the same way.

Since we were all done with him, it was the Queen's turn. The Queen asked one of the guards to pull Emma's honey-soaked underwear out of his mouth, so he would be able to talk. He tried to bite the guard as he did so, and the guard quickly hit him in the head with his rifle.

"Ouch!" the Evil UnBearded Bee Man said angrily. The Queen moved to stand directly in front of the man, in the middle of the circle. Two guards stood with her, one on each side. The double doors suddenly opened and four guards entered the room, rolling a phone booth-type of contraption between them. It was large, about eight feet tall, and appeared to be one of those machines used on game shows, where the contestant goes inside and after the door closes, paper money blows all over the place. Whatever cash the person can catch, is theirs to keep. As the guards placed the large booth next to the sticky, honey-covered Evil Unbearded Bee Man, I noticed the booth had a small glass door on the front that was slightly open. Two more guards then entered the room with another booth of the same type, only it wasn't as large. It too had a small glass window in the front, slightly open. They placed it a few feet in front of the Evil UnBearded Bee Man. The Queen then turned and faced him and said, "Today you will feel almost as much pain as my girls felt, when you raped each of them. That's what happens to people who rape and murder children."

"I never personally murdered any children; only raped," said the Evil UnBearded Bee Man.

"The word 'only' should never be used before the word 'raped', you bastard. You are a murderer, and because of your actions, I had no choice but to have my own child, the Princess, 'accidentally' murdered. The Evil UnBearded Bee Man looked confused.

"For fuck's sake, what are you talking about?" He asked angrily. "You're not making any sense at all, you old bat. How could me raping anyone, lead to the murder of the Princess?" Before the Queen could answer, one of her guards hit him in the head with his rifle, again, for calling the Queen 'an old bat'. The Queen then spoke, as the Evil Unbearded Bee Man squinted in pain.

"When you decided to ruin your life by choosing to live a life of crime, your rape of *me* resulted in a pregnancy. I gave my daughter up for adoption, because I wanted no reminders of you. My son fell in love with the Princess and married her, without knowing they were related. She was his half-sister. I didn't realize who she was, until after she had their third child. So, I had to have her and my three grandchildren killed, because of *you*. I could not have those children suffer with diseases or abnormalities because of what you did to me."

The Evil UnBearded Bee Man looked confused again. "You didn't have to kill them," he said.

"It was a tough decision," the Queen replied. "But, I will not have the public talk about my grandchildren as diseased. That is not royalty! Now, look at all the damage you have done. It doesn't seem fair that one person could ruin so many lives, and I will put an end to that today. "Guards!" she then yelled. "Bring her in!" The Evil UnBearded Bee Man looked past the Queen to see his daughter being escorted in with force, by two very strong guards.

"Sammy!" he yelled.

"Daddy?" Sam cried. The guards escorted her into the smaller of the two booths, in front of her father, and all of us girls lined up with newly filled cups of honey in our hands. The Queen had quietly informed me a few minutes before, to have all of us girls go out to the buckets of watered-down honey and get full cups. One by one, each of us girls poured our cup of honey on Sam. Not too many of us had any words for her. I heard mumbles of, "You dug your own grave", "You deserve this" and "Who's the bully now?" I would have expected an answer from Sam. But, then again, it's kind of hard to speak with a mouthful of honey. Once we were done and Sam was covered in honey, one of the guards shut the large door on the side, so she was sealed in, and opened the small glass door in the front.

I wanted to say something to Sam, but I didn't. I was trying to digest what the Queen had said moments before. The Queen had been raped by the same man, had birthed his child, and had then given her up for adoption. Then, the Prince had fallen in love with his half-sister, married her and had children. When the Queen figured out who the Princess was, she had felt forced to have her and her own grandchildren killed, so no one in her "perfect royal family" would discover the truth, if the real reason behind any birth defects or abnormalities in one of the children was the result of incest between siblings. That was a big pill to swallow. I was certainly at a loss for words.

The double doors opened, and two more guards came in, each holding a beehive. The beehives had a hole in each of them, with a tube attached. At the end of each tube was a plastic cover. You could hear the bees buzzing, loudly. Both guards walked toward Sammy's booth and stopped in front of it. Another guard stepped forward and took off the plastic covers off the end of the tubes of both beehives and positioned the tubes inside the small glass window. Thousands of bees went flying into the booth with Sam. As soon as all the bees were in the booth, one of the guards closed the window. Her father stood there and watched in despair, as a single tear rolled down his face. Sam screamed bloody murder for five minutes. Then, there was dead silence. It was hard to witness someone get eaten alive. I was sure she could have lived a better life, if it hadn't been for the way she was raised. Two more guards walked in with beehives. As they headed toward the larger booth, the two guards who had been guarding Sam's father, escorted him into the larger booth. As soon as he stepped in, they shut the large side door and sealed it. He didn't resist.

"Here we go again," he mumbled, as a guard positioned the two tubes into the opening of the small glass window of the booth. Those were the last words Joseph Gonzalez spoke before his death. The last thing he got to see was his daughter die slowly, right before his eyes, and there was zero he could do about it. He had chosen the wrong person to mess with. The Queen always won. She was not a force to reckon with, and she sure knew how to get revenge. I loved, but also hated the decisions she had made. The Queen then spoke.

"Alright, girls. The show is over. Go get ready for dinner." She spoke in such a calm voice, as if nothing had just happened. It was simply time to move on and never speak of it again. I was not expecting that. But, what was done was done, and nothing could change it. We all left the room in silence, and got ready for dinner. After dinner was finished, the Queen asked for tea with honey. She had never requested that before. She always drank coffee. Maybe she just needed to say the word, 'honey'.

I have experienced so much in my life. I will never have all the answers as to how life can get so crazy. I can never figure out people. You think you know somebody, but you only know what they want you to know. We never know each other's innermost thoughts. If we did, I think the world would be worse than it already is. I have been on many journeys. I have traveled, and I've moved around way too many times. I have lived in cardboard boxes, on friends' couches, in small apartments, and in rented rooms in strangers' homes, to back to the high life living with the Queen's double doors. When you live behind double doors, the outside can tell you're wealthy. But, what goes on behind those closed double doors could make your head spin. I had to grow up too fast and I didn't get to enjoy my childhood as much as I wanted to. But, it's safe to say I did things *my way*, even if it was sometimes the wrong way.

I have worked hard, but I have also been very lazy at times. I've abused alcohol, driven drunk, been arrested, have helped saved lives, and I've loved getting stoned and having the munchies. I've never tried heavy duty drugs like heroin, like some of my friends did. But, it is safe to say, I've had many good times, great friends, horrific enemies, and a dysfunctional family. Now that I am getting older, I have to say my life has become quite boring.

I despise being like one of those people who just goes to work, returns home and makes dinner, and then watches TV. Then, on some Friday nights, goes to Bingo. I want to keep writing and using my imagination. Like many others, I have had my heart broken. I've cried tears of joy, tears of pain, and I've laughed so hard that my underwear got a little damp. I've had three-day hangovers, blackouts, surgeries and hearing loss. If I could do it all over again, I'd try to avoid a lot of the trouble I got myself into, and I would certainly try to escape being the victim of some very bad things.

I've given up on trying to impress people, and I've stopped caring about what people think of me. I care more about animals than people, because I am addicted to unconditional love. That is something I currently only find with my dog, Dakota. Everybody else, except for who I consider family and friends, can "live and let live, or live and let die". I'm half and half: a very nice, loyal and sweet girl, but I also have evil and mean wishes for anyone who doubles crosses me. I would jump into a fire to save someone, because I am brave. But, I will also run like a scared little child, if I see a spider. Everyone has their own stories to tell, but for some reason they bore me. I am trying to change my ways and thoughts, since I have failed in more relationships, than succeeded. It is safe to say though, I am always able to smile, even if I am crying inside.

I moved out of the Queen's house, after I watched those two people die right before my eyes, and learned of the Queen murdering her own daughter and grandchildren. Whatever her reasons were, it just didn't sit well for me. Living on the streets, without a job, just going to the library for shelter to type up more books makes me somewhat happy.

I went from rags to riches, and then from riches to rags. I do miss the security of living behind double doors. But, I am almost fifty years old, with a maximum of about fifty years more to live. I must live within my means, and my means really do suck.

Getting off subject again, I think of what to write day and night, and I pray my readers want more. I am so excited to publish this book. My fingers are crossed in the hopes this book sells many copies. I pray to get a lot of positive feedback, as well. If I do, I will certainly write books for a living, Time will tell. I hope the rest I am thinking of writing isn't boring. I voluntarily left the Queen's home, knowing I could not return for a minimum of ten years. I had put up with so much mental abuse from her, yet I had still looked up to her. I would have preferred physical abuse, because that pain goes away. The mental scars have remained forever in my heart and mind. I am a tough, but very sensitive girl, who cries myself to sleep way too often. I still looked up to the Queen, regardless of her actions, causes and effects. To me, she was my mama and papa all in one person. Even though I had lived in this huge palace with my siblings, I only saw them at meal times. We never discussed our feelings, and our relationship simply fizzled away. I had to leave there and try and make it out in the real world, all alone. I couldn't live with a murderer, regardless if the victims deserved to die. That is up to *my* God, not the Queen. I think what bothers me the most, is she gave us the option to watch. Even though it was my choice, it still gives me nightmares.

With the small amount of pounds I had left in my bank account, for doing chores, I booked a flight back to the United States. I was hoping to start a new life, and debated whether I should contact my relatives, who thought I was dead. I finally decided to visit my Aunt Sue. When I arrived, I noticed a different last name on her mailbox. I almost walked away, but then wondered if maybe she had gotten married. When I rang the bell, an old man answered. I asked if anyone named Susan still lived there.

He said, "No, she moved several years ago, and she didn't leave a forwarding address." I thanked him for his time and walked away. With nowhere else to go and little funds, I rented a smelly, furnished room with my service dog Dakota; a room I had seen advertised on Craigslist. I could have gone back to my sisters, or tried to find my brother in England, but I chose not to. I got a job at a family-owned aviation company. I worked there for a few years and became close with many of my co-workers; especially Dyanne Sapanaro, who I nicknamed Bubba, as well as Michelle West, Nicole Kent, Carolyn Mumme (may she rest in peace), Darlene Scalara and Lynn Hines, whose nickname was Lynn-Lynn. X-person, Tricia (may she rest in peace), Paul Cooperman (may he rest in peace), Cathy Guhl, Terri and Kelly Lloyd, Frances Veltri… The list goes on. They were all like family to me, especially the owners, the Levi's. It wasn't just a job, it was like having a family. Yes, I had another (at times) dysfunctional family. Second to Betty, I was the most dysfunctional. Even if everything was fine, Betty would invent things to complain about. We all knew each other so well, it could be good or bad at times, because we knew way too much about each other. One thing was for sure though, no matter what happened in our love-hate relationships, if something was wrong, there was always someone there for you at work to help. It broke my heart when my boss Andrew Levi suddenly passed away. It could have been prevented, if he told us he was sick. But, he had chosen not to. He didn't like doctors at all. He was like a brother to me, and he is missed by so many. The company closed shortly after his death. It was heartbreaking, and I still think of it every now and then. It's so true, you don't know what you have until it's gone.

Everything seemed to go downhill after Andy's death. It changed so many people's lives, but we all had to find a way to move on. Some did it quicker than others. I, for one, will never forget him or that job. It was like losing another family. I was homeless for a while, and thank God for Karen Kincaid and Marima (Meemaw) for taking me in. I am also grateful for my sister and her husband, for making sure I was indoors with Dakota. The winters get pretty cold. Willie Wilson, Larry Sharkey, Mike Mudder, Tyson Adams, Diana and Bobby Steele, Kevin Carney, David Wamsley, Smurf, Connie Lewis, Steve Siegel, Alicia Brady plus many others went above and beyond to help me during difficult times. And believe you me, I had to ask for favors and I hated doing that! I am more of a giver. I also must thank my friends: Anne Brown, Michele Shock, Matt Shock and family, plus my nephew Jason Pesch, and Kerri-Bell, and last, but not least, my Dr. Wilkens, because I would never make it through life without my prescribed Xanax. I know this is not the acknowledgement part of the book, but since they've done so much for me, I just had to mention them *in* the book, or I could suffer some major consequences! LOL.

Moving on, there was a time in my life when I had certainly picked the wrong crowd of people to become friends with. I chose to hang out with people who drank a lot of alcohol and smoked a lot of pot. I got in trouble with the law on several occasions. The name on my fake passport, my new identity I had been given as a child, was Chelsey Williams. When I received my third DUI, I reluctantly played the only card I had, to keep my sorry ass out of jail. I certainly hated it there. Peeing and pooping in front of a cell-mate. Eww, eww, eww! When I say something three times, I really mean it! Those had been the worst two days of my life, when I had been taken to jail for my second DUI. I really wish I wasn't the type who didn't like rules, but it's hard to change your true self. I knew I was not allowed to ask the Queen for help, since it had been less than ten years since I had relocated. Plus, telling her would probably be a worse punishment than the Court system.

So, when I got my third DUI, I made the decision to tell the police my real name, instead of the one on my fake passport. I revealed that I was one of the victims in the Underground Fort rape case. That opened a whole new can of worms. Allegedly, the police and higher authorities were the only one who knew about the fake murder massacre. They had taken my handcuffs off, as I was coming off my buzz. They put me in a room with a large oval table, and told me to sit and wait there for a private detective. A few hours later, Detective Murphy showed up. He looked a lot older, with more white hair. They chose him to be the one to talk to me, to see if I looked familiar, even though many years had passed. He recognized me right away, but to be sure, he asked me questions that he knew only the victims of the underground fort rape case would know the correct answers to. After he confirmed it was me, he was very friendly. He asked how I was doing and what my life had been like for the past couple of years. I told him it had been like a roller coaster, as far as some ups and downs.

He said he was extremely busy, because his friend was in the hospital, but he would try to get the charges against me dropped. But, I first needed to go for a ride with him to talk to some people. I was skeptical. Something didn't feel right, but I went with him anyway. We drove for about an hour, and I knew I had to get away. It was a gut feeling I couldn't shake off. I asked him if he could please pull over, because my doggie Dakota needed to do her business. He agreed, not suspecting anything, and pulled over exactly where I wanted him to, three blocks away from the Fox 5 Television Studio. The second I got out of the car, holding Dakota, I took off running as fast as I could. I liked Detective Murphy, but I had to go with my gut feeling. Murphy screamed for me to stop, but I trusted my instincts and keep running. I think Murphy had been planning to have me somehow disappear, maybe even have me committed to a mental institution, so no one would ever believe anything I ever had to say.

Everyone is born with some sort of power, whether it be psychic, having premonitions, seeing ghosts, et cetera. Some people are more in tune with those things than others, and other people don't believe in any of it. I know for sure I was blessed with two. I can feel when something is not right, and I always seem to sense when a specific person is thinking about or talking about me, or is going to contact me soon. The second is, I can feel if a house is haunted by one or more spirits, and I know if it's an evil spirit, or just a spirit who is curious or confused. I felt that being in Murphy's car was not a good place to be, so I have escaped the second I had the chance.

I ran as fast as a possibly could, because I knew he would call for back-up. I must have run three miles past the studio, as that would have been too obvious of a place to find me. I ended up at a small church next to a library. The church was empty, so I decided to hide there and sleep since there was a pretty good hiding place behind the stage. The next morning, Dakota howled and woke me up because she heard someone enter the church. I heard a voice say, "Who's there?" I got up and saw a man at the door. I apologized and told him I would explain. I walked up to him near the door, hatching my escape plan as I approached him. I said, "Hello, my name is--" Then, ran out the door with Dakota, back the way I had come from the day before. He didn't chase after me.

I took back roads, until I saw the large sign high in the air, that read, *Fox 5 News.* I waited by the entrance, since I wasn't sure it was unlocked. Maybe only an employee with a badge or a key could open it. I didn't want to draw attention to myself by yanking on a locked door. I stood near the entrance, over in a grassy area with Dakota, acting as if I had just brought her outside to do her business. Within a few minutes, someone pulled up and parked and then opened the door and walked inside. As soon as they entered, I caught the open door, took a deep breath and held Dakota close to me as we entered. I went to the front desk and the receptionist said no dogs were allowed in the building. I pulled out Dakota's service dog identification and she agreed Dakota was fine to accompany me, and asked how she could help me. I asked if I could speak to a reporter, because I had a story they would consider breaking news. She told me to have a seat.

About thirty minutes later, a male reporter came out and shook my hand, and invited me and Dakota into his office. I told him the truth, and explained that even though I may be listed as a woman fleeing from the law, that was a lie. I told him I was one of the victims from a story that had occurred over ten years before, the Underground Fort rape case.

"I know it sounds like old news, but not everything is as it appeared," I said to him. "I can supply all the proof you need, that none of those little girls were murdered at the school. We were all taken overseas to a relocation center, along with our parents and siblings, to protect us from the Joseph Gonzalez's gang, that wanted us dead. The local police and the FBI, along with the CIA, have done a great job of protecting us and keeping us all safe. But, I've been able to save enough to tell my story to you... if your price is right. I hate to rat them out because they saved my life, but I am totally broke. So, I've decided to sell my story. I need to be able to feed my dog, and take her to a veterinarian for a check-up." The reporter looked at me for a few long seconds.

"What kind of proof do you have?" he asked.

"I have a video, two copies of it on flash drives in safety deposit boxes, at two different banks. A third copy is well-hidden, in case you narc me out. I also have some videos on my cell phone, of all the other girls who were victims in the case. I secretly taped us all talking about it, in our group therapy."

He asked if I was willing to take a DNA test, to prove I was who I said I was, and not just some gal who broke the law and was making up a story to get out of trouble. He said the news station had run a story about me the night before, along with every other news station in the area, and I was wanted by the police. I agreed to the DNA test, and told him I would also sign anything as long as I was allowed to have a lawyer look over the documents first.

"My gut tells me you're telling the truth," he said. "And, believe it or not, you are not the only gal who has come forward with the same story. But, she has disappeared. I want this story. Don't speak to anyone else. You can use my computer and phone. Call a lawyer. Do what you need to do, and I'll be back in an hour or so. Help yourself to coffee or water, and I'll bring you a bowl for water for your dog."

"Thank you," I said. I was relieved, but not letting my guard down. "Please tell me you're not calling the police to take me away." He gave me his word.

Ten minutes later, Detective Murphy appeared in the doorway to take Dakota and I in.

"I thought you retired," I said, sarcastically. I hated that reporter.

"Well, life got boring, so I decided to be on call," Detective Murphy said. "I know you knew things weren't going to go good for you, and that's why you ran. You are smart, Laura. But, we are smarter. I cannot allow you or any of the other girls who have come back here to the United States, to put our reputation and jobs on the line, for trying to save your lives. I understand your life hasn't been a picnic. I don't know all the details of what occurred over in England. I have the power to take your dog away because of your disloyalty, but I like you. So, I will pull some strings and not separate you and Dakota. You will be living in a mental hospital, with the other victims who tried to get the story out…" *I knew it!* I thought. *They're going to make everyone believe we're all crazy.*

"It's much better there, then in prison," he continued. "But, if you try to pull a fast one, they will put you in maximum security and will medicate you so heavily, you'll barely be able to feed your own dog. So, take my advice and behave yourself, and keep your mouth shut." I didn't answer him. I just nodded as my eyes filled with tears. He put us in his car and about twenty minutes later, I was being admitted into the mental hospital. I didn't say goodbye to Detective Murphy, when he apologized and said goodbye. I made sure he saw my devastated face, as I was led away.

After they locked me and Dakota in a room by ourselves for a few hours, they let us out to go to group therapy. I saw a lot of the girls I had lived with in England for so many years, and I was relieved when they all seemed somewhat happy to see me. I was glad they weren't given any kind of medication to erase their memories. They were all sitting in a circle and had left my space open, for me to sit. Deja-vu, once again. There were no counselors there.

"When did each of you leave the Palace, and why?" I asked. They explained, they had always followed my lead, and had a feeling when I left that I would go to the media. So, they had left to try to find me and one by one, had ended up going to the media themselves. All of them had somehow, in some way, ended up here. "I am so sorry. I got us into this mess, but I'll get us out," I said. "I'll find a way to get in touch with the Queen. She has much more power than any of the United States authorities. Raise your hand if you're on board." Every girl raised their hand.

TO BE CONTINUED...

LETTER FROM THE AUTHOR

I worked very hard on this book, and put all my eggs in this basket. I really hope to get some fans. If not, I will figure out a plan B. I am unemployed and staying with family members. I kind of feel like a loser, because I have made so many bad choices and mistakes in my life. I am trying to better myself as I am getting older. But, there's still a wild child in me! Maybe one day I will grow up. We shall see. I am forty-five years old, and feel like my ducks will never be in a row. Writing is my passion and I hope it becomes my full-time career. Thanks for reading this, and it sure was happy writing for me.

I'd like to give an extra special thanks to Emma Michaels, for helping me finalize and format this book, and teaching me about self-publishing and promotion. From one kidney donor to another, you rock!

I would also like to thank all those people who have helped me through my writing journey. If I've accidentally left anyone out, you can yell at me on Facebook and I will include you in my next book, if I am blessed enough to get readers to write a part two. I have been writing my whole life, but unfortunately, all my books, poems and song lyrics were ruined by flood waters caused by a hurricane. I didn't let that stop me, though. I wrote another novel, but that one was also ruined by a flood. That flood was my fault though, because as I was cleaning one day, I moved a heavy rolled up carpet and put it on top of a washing machine hose. Well, the hose slowly cracked open while I was sleeping. I woke up to see my sneakers floating in water, instead of the floor, and I thought it was a dream.

I was about to throw in the towel on writing, but decided the third time could be the charm. Plus, now there are flash-drives. I am old school, but am trying to be a successful writer and hope to do this full-time. I'm even working on getting a blog and a website up and running. I do hope you all enjoyed my writing, so I am able to pursue my dream of making a living as a full-time writer. It all depends on how this book does. My email address is jersiegirl225@yahoo.com, if any of you have any questions, or if you'd like updates on any future book releases, or if you'd like to know when my blog and website are active. Please feel free to contact me via my email address. I'm looking forward to it!

Warmest Regards,

Laura May

The Absent Kids by Laura May Fleming

Published by Laura May Fleming

Cover by: Marc "with a C" Fleming

Kindle Paperback ISBN: 9781677943876

Made in the USA
Monee, IL
27 January 2021